Breakfast
New Mexico Style

Breakfast
New Mexico Style

**A Dining Guide to More
Than 100 Favorite, Fancy,
Funky & Family Friendly Restaurants**

with over
80 Librarian- Recommended Books
& Many Fun After-Breakfast Activities

Valerie Nye & Kathy Barco

SUNSTONE
PRESS

SANTA FE

Sunstone books may be purchased for educational, business, or sales promotional use.
For information please write: Special Markets Department, Sunstone Press,
P.O. Box 2321, Santa Fe, New Mexico 87504-2321.

Book design ►Vicki Ahl
Body typeface ► Arial ◄► Display typeface ►RNM_Pecos
Printed on acid free paper

Library of Congress Cataloging-in-Publication Data

Nye, Valerie, 1971-
  Breakfast New Mexico style : a dining guide to more than 100 favorite, fancy, funky and family
friendly restaurants with over 80 librarian-recommended books and many fun after-breakfast
activities / by Valerie Nye & Kathy Barco.
      p. cm.
  Includes bibliographical references.
  ISBN 978-0-86534-716-8 (softcover : alk. paper)
  1. Restaurants--New Mexico--Guidebooks. 2. Breakfasts--New Mexico. I. Barco, Kathy,
1946- II. Title.
  TX907.3.N6N94 2009
  647.959789--dc22
                              2009010279

Published in

WWW.SUNSTONEPRESS.COM
SUNSTONE PRESS / POST OFFICE BOX 2321 / SANTA FE, NM 87504-2321 /USA
(505) 988-4418 / ORDERS ONLY (800) 243-5644 / FAX (505) 988-1025

To Mike Jaynes
Breakfast
just isn't the same without you.

Acknowledgements

It may be true that too many cooks spoil a broth, but too many librarians definitely enrich a book when they combine their research skills and appetites to cook up reviews of their favorite breakfast restaurants. See who these talented and well-fed folks are in the Contributors section of this book. *Muchas gracias.*

We also wish to thank Jeanne-Marie Bakehouse, Chris Clark, Relf Price, and Mary Lou Sullenberger, who tastefully pointed out errors and inconsistencies in the final manuscript. Any mistakes that escaped their sharp eyes are strictly the fault of the authors, and we will dutifully eat our words.

"When you wake up in the morning, Pooh," said Piglet at last, "what's the first thing you say to yourself?"

"What's for breakfast?" said Pooh. "What do you say, Piglet?"

"I say, I wonder what's going to happen exciting today?" said Piglet.

Pooh nodded thoughtfully. "It's the same thing," he said.

—A. A. Milne, *The House at Pooh Corner*

Also by Kathy Barco and Valerie Nye:

Breakfast Santa Fe Style – A Fancy, Funky, and Family Friendly Dining Guide to Santa Fe Restaurants, 2007 New Mexico Book Award Finalist, Travel/Guidebook Category

Here's what some of the authors whose books were mentioned in the "recommended reading" had to say about *Breakfast Santa Fe Style:*

Visitors (and even old-hand Santa Feans) can learn a lot from "Breakfast Santa Fe Style". It takes you from A (Adelita's Mexican Restaurant) to Z (Zia Diner) with 55 other eating places in between and describes not just menus but the ambience.

— Tony Hillerman

Breakfast Santa Fe Style is a wonderful guide to good food and good books. Other than great sex, what can be better than that?

— Michael McGarrity

The format, the fun writing style and the detailed and artful content make me want to try every restaurant and read every book. It's such an interesting read cover to cover!

— Ana Baca

I was surprised to learn from this guide that shopping for breakfast in historic Santa Fe can be quite an adventure. The authors recommend eateries and I recommend their book.

— Marc Simmons

You have written a book that is informative, lively, practical, and tasty. Congratulations! Breakfast is the most important meal of the day, and should never involve surprises. You have taken the surprise out of breakfast in Santa Fe and, in its place, you have given us many nutritious alternatives for reading besides the morning newspaper with its appetite suppressing headlines.

— Marc Talbert

The best and cheapest way to see your friends is to go to breakfast together on a sunlit Santa Fe morning. Kathy & Valerie present a menu of wonderful places to enjoy with friends, including the 4th of July Pancake Feast on the Plaza with the whole town either cooking or eating or dancing or parading.

— Barbara Beasley Murphy

Contents

Introduction

In 2008, after attending a session celebrating libraries at the New Mexico State Legislature, we enjoyed a late breakfast at Tía Sophia's in downtown Santa Fe. Between sips of coffee and bites of *huevos rancheros,* we brainstormed ways to follow up the success of our award-winning 2006 book, *Breakfast Santa Fe Style.* Breakfast would still be our focus, and we wanted to cover as much of New Mexico as possible. We decided to enlist our library colleagues, many of whom had expressed dismay that we hadn't involved them in the "research" for our first book. With all of these ingredients in mind, *Breakfast New Mexico Style* was born.

After breakfast we rushed to our computers and began sending out invitations. We contacted librarians in New Mexico's big and small communities. Their assignment was to visit their favorite local restaurants, eat breakfast, and write about their experiences. We received a virtual buffet of passionate reviews, and added a few of our own. The final mouth-watering task was to compile and edit the submissions. Things came together like a perfect omelet.

Since all of the people who contributed to this book were connected with libraries, they were more than happy to recommend a book or two to go along with each review. We have also included fun and interesting places to visit after breakfast.

In memory of Mike Jaynes, the designer and ardent supporter of *Breakfast Santa Fe Style*, a percentage of the royalties from *Breakfast New Mexico Style* will go to the New Mexico Library Foundation (NMLF). The NMLF is a non-profit organization that supports public, school, academic, and special libraries statewide. For more information about the NMLF, visit www.nm-lf.org

Whether you're in New Mexico for the first time, a returning visitor, or a longtime resident of New Mexico, we hope you'll savor this book. We have included a wide variety of places, including bakeries, burrito stands, and elegant restaurants.

There are so many exciting breakfast options in New Mexico. Traditional foods include tortillas, beans, eggs, *chorizo* (red sausage), and red and green chile. These tasty elements serve as a palette for New Mexico's artistic cooks and chefs. Creative cooks mix and match ingredients to make a wide variety of breakfast dishes. Offerings start with the traditional burrito and Mexican omelet, but can range to wildly imaginative breakfast sandwiches and the hands down, no doubt about it, most incredibly named menu item: the Hen Grenade. Breakfast in New Mexico can easily be the most memorable meal of the day.

Pricing:

$ Average cost for entrée less than $6

$$ Average cost for entrée $6-$10

$$$ Average cost for entrée $11 and up

Kid Component:

*   Children welcome, but not an easy restaurant for children and all of their needs

**   The restaurant can easily accommodate one or more children at a table

*** Children have their own menu and the restaurant can easily accommodate one or more children at a table

Notes from the Editors:

We are Valerie and Kathy, your taste bud tour guides. We grew up in New Mexico, left the state for college and careers, and are lucky enough to have returned to the Land of Enchantment. We have terrific friends, colleagues, and acquaintances who work hard to provide library services to people all over our great state. In honor of the profession in which we all serve, we have included recommended reading with each restaurant description.

Some Things to Keep in Mind:

Although several of the restaurants listed in this book have websites, we've learned not to count on the accuracy of the information posted there, especially concerning menu items and hours of operation. Please be aware that restaurants often change menus, prices, décor, and even location. The information in this book is current as of 2009. We will also post updates on our website: www. breakfastnewmexicostyle.com

Many of the restaurants serve alcohol at breakfast, except on Sundays when you'll have to wait until noon to enjoy that mimosa.

Be prepared for New Mexico's official state question: "red or green?" It refers to which type of chile you would like to have with your meal. If you're not sure, you can ask for both and specify "on the side." That way you can taste for yourself and determine your preference. Most places tend to serve your meal "smothered" in whatever sauce you choose. You can avoid some potential dining disasters by being picky at first. Don't worry about offending your server and asking for chile on the side. Just think of how Sally ordered her food in the movie *When Harry Met Sally*.

Above all, enjoy sampling the saucy, subtle, spicy, sweet, succulent flavors of Breakfast New Mexico Style!

Abiquiú

Café Abiquiú

21120 Highway 84
Abiquiú, NM 87510
(888) 735-2902
www.abiquiuinn.com/cafe.htm

Breakfast hours:
Daily 7:30am-11am
(April-November)
Kid component:**
Price: $$

The area around Abiquiú has attracted living creatures for an unimaginable amount of time. Dinosaurs walked the swampy lands that made up this patch of land over 200 million years ago. Native American settlements are estimated to have begun in this valley in the 1200s. In the mid 1930s Georgia O'Keeffe began her visits to the Abiquiú area, eventually making her home in the valley.

When you visit Abiquiú today, you will find the spiritual beauty that has attracted people and creatures to this area since the beginning of time. The perfect place to stop on your visit through this sacred land is the Café Abiquiú, located in the Abiquiú Inn just south of the village of Abiquiú.

The Café is a comfortable morning stop, well worth a drive from Santa Fe, Española, and even Albuquerque. Large windows allow views of the trees and gardens surrounding the café. With the hum of conversation and never-ending hot coffee, this is a slow-paced restaurant where you will feel comfortable spending an hour or more before heading off on your day of adventures.

Café Abiquiú has an extensive and exciting breakfast menu with entrées inspired by traditional Northern New Mexico foods. Most entrées include corn, blue corn, and *pico de gallo*. The Sunrise Over Chama Valley includes two corn cakes with eggs, avocado, and *pico de gallo*. Cerro Pedernal is a stack of corn cakes with fresh strawberries, cream cheese, and almonds. The "Paint Your Omelet" selection is an option that allows you to build your own omelet just the way you like it. On the lighter side you might turn your gaze toward oatmeal (it comes with raisins, walnuts, and brown sugar) or the parfait (yogurt with fruit and granola). On our visits we have also enjoyed the Lil' Abiquiú (pan fried trout served with eggs) and the classic New Mexico entrée, *huevos rancheros*.

A relatively large gift shop is located adjacent to the café. There you will find weavings, photography, jewelry, and paintings created by local artists. Books about New Mexico and the Abiquiú area are also available.

Recommended Reading: Lesley Poling-Kempes beautifully recounts the wandering ancient and recent history of Ghost Ranch in her book entitled *Ghost Ranch*. In this book you will read about dinosaurs, artists, business entrepreneurs, children, animals, and airplane pilots and how they all had an impact on this area of the world.

After Breakfast: Head 15 miles north on Highway 84 and turn right at Ghost Ranch. Visitors are welcome at this retreat run by the Presbyterian Church. You can hike, shop for creations made by local artisans, and visit three museums.
www.ghostranch.org

Albuquerque Area

Asbury Café

Main Street
Expo New Mexico
(New Mexico State Fair)
300 San Pedro Blvd. NE
Albuquerque, NM 87108
www.exponm.com

Breakfast Hours: Daily during the Fair in September (check website for dates)
Kid Component:*
Price: $

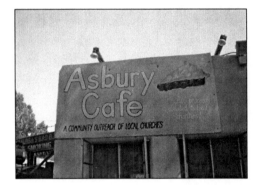

If the idea of pie for breakfast sounds heavenly to you, join the line of the faithful who make an annual pilgrimage to the Asbury Café. A State Fair tradition since 1960, the fare at the Asbury tops many folks' lists of "favorite State Fair food," beating out the more mundane funnel cake, corn on the cob, turkey legs, and even deep-fried Oreos for sale at other food booths. Eating pie can be an almost spiritual experience, and the fact that all the Asbury's proceeds are donated to local charities makes upgrading to "à la mode" seem more like a blessing than a calorie count. The Asbury gives a whole new meaning to the term piety.

The hardest part of a visit to the Asbury is making up your mind. There are just too many choices. All eyes are focused on the "Asbury Pie Menu" hanging from the ceiling inside the small building or beside the walk-up window outside. This semi-high-tech sign features the names of 36 varieties of pies with a red light beside each one. Here's the key to the light show: "Light On = We Have It; Light Flashing = Almost Sold Out; Light Off = Sorry - All Gone." The usual suspects are on the list: Apple, Blueberry, Cherry, Peach, and Pecan. Then there are the combos: Apple Nut Raisin, Blackberry/Apricot, and Strawberry/

Rhubarb are a few of the matches seemingly made in heaven. Hungry for a hybrid? Try Oatmeal/Chocolate Chip, Brownie/Reeses, or Cranberry/Apple. Many pie fans swear by the Shoofly. And, if you have special dietary needs, you're in luck: sugar-free and gluten-free pies are also on the menu!

What's that you say? You're not in the mood for a sweet pie? Don't despair, the Asbury has tempting non-dessert items. A highly trustworthy official in the nearby Home Arts building has told us on more than one occasion that the Asbury Café's Frito Chili Pie is the best on the fairgrounds. The café itself has limited inside seating, but there are plenty of picnic tables outside the door, all the better to observe Fair-goers.

If you happen to over-indulge and feel the need to stretch your legs, there's plenty of stuff to see at the Fair; walking around to gawk is excellent exercise. And just think…once the Fair ends, you'll have almost a whole year to slim down before September rolls around and it's Asbury time again.

Recommended Reading: 2008 was the 70th anniversary of the New Mexico State Fair. To see what the fair was like in earlier days, invest some time perusing the plethora of photographs in *State Fair! The Biggest Show in New Mexico* by Wade McIntyre, published in 1995. You might even see someone you know in these photographs. We did!

After Breakfast: The only sensible thing to do after eating pie for breakfast is to head out into the crowds at the State Fair. Just east of the Asbury Café is the Creative Arts/Home Arts Building. It's fun to wander through and admire the Lego creations, crafts, quilts, and needlework on display. If you plan your visit right, you could watch the judging of a food contest. Who knows? Seeing all of those mouth watering creations might send you back for another piece of pie!

Barelas Coffee House

1502 4th St SW
Albuquerque, NM 87102
(505) 843-7577

Breakfast Hours:
Monday-Friday 7:30am-3pm,
Saturday 7:30am-2:30pm
Kid Component:++
Prices: $$

The Barelas Coffee House is in the Barelas neighborhood, one of the original villages that make up old downtown Albuquerque. It is situated on South Fourth Street, a road of many histories from the time of El Camino Real connecting Spanish settlements to the more recent eras of Historic US Route 66 and US 85. The railroad yards are on the east, with the Rio Grande on the west.

Many who come to the Coffee House for breakfast are regulars. Likewise, many of the serving staff have been there for years and they greet individuals and families as more than mere acquaintances. Patrons from all over the metro area and surrounding rural communities frequent this restaurant. Leaders from Albuquerque's educational institutions, governments, and churches are often seen here, greeting old friends and fellow patrons from nearby neighborhoods and downtown businesses who return to visit the old community of Barelas. City Councilors and officials including the Mayor, Bernalillo County officials, members of the Fire and Police Departments, NM State Officials and Legislators, along with the Governor and members of the New Mexican Congressional contingent, are all likely to be spotted at this restaurant, mixing with business people, lawyers, contractors, subcontractors, city workers, laborers, teachers, and even an occasional librarian.

The food is central and northern New Mexican with distinctive red or green chile and consistently well-prepared *frijoles*. Breakfast features these distinctive ingredients in egg burritos, *huevos rancheros*, and *carne adovada* and eggs. Eggs with bacon, sausage, or ham are also on the breakfast menu; pancakes are available until ll:00 am.

Huevos rancheros deluxe with corn tortillas and cheese is an irresistible favorite. In addition, at any time steaming New Mexican dishes of *menudo*, *posolé*, and red or green chile with beans may pass by your table to be served to nearby diners.

Over the years, many people return to the Barelas Coffee House and to the community of Barelas. The musically inclined will find this returning motif as part of the narrative structure of the opera *Time and Again Barelas*. It was composed by Miguel del Aguila for the New Mexico Symphony's performance contribution to the 2006 Tricentennial Celebration of the founding of Albuquerque.

Recommended Reading: A book that highlights the geographical, political, and cultural attributes that define the Coffee House is Rudolfo Anaya's novel *Alburquerque*. The Rio Grande River and the community of Barelas figure prominently in the book. One banker character reminisces: "'Order us a bowl of green chile stew,' don Manuel says when we have lunch at the Petroleum Club, slapping me on the back and roaring with laughter. He knows we don't get any chile there or at the Rotary lunches…But on days when we need our chile fix we go down to Barelas…and sit and eat two or three bowlsful of the hottest stuff we can get. Then we remember the old days."

After Breakfast: Just to the south of the Barelas Coffee House at the intersection of Avenida César Chávez (Bridge Boulevard) and 4th Street SW is the National Hispanic Cultural Center. Opened in 2000, the NHCC is dedicated to the preservation, promotion, and advancement of Hispanic culture, arts, and humanities.
www.nationalhispaniccenter.org

Calico Café

6855 4th St. NW
Albuquerque, NM 87107
(505) 890-9150
www.calicocafellc.com

Breakfast Hours:
Friday-Sunday 7:30am-2pm,
Monday-Thursday
11am-2pm
Monday 7:30am-2pm,
Tuesday-Sunday 7:30am-9pm
Kid Component:***
Prices: $$

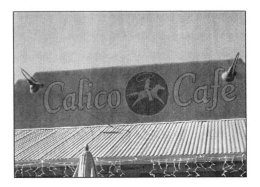

Cowgirl cakes, cowgirl benedicts—see a theme? The menu (with artwork by Doreman Burns) and the atmosphere let you know that Vernon and Angel Garcia are giving a mighty tip of the hat to those hard-working women of the ranch at their North Valley restaurant, Calico Café.

The Calico Café was first located in Corrales, but in December of 2004 the popular and intimate lunch and breakfast restaurant was consumed by fire. In 2006, the Garcias grabbed the reins and turned southwest, purchasing the old Sal's Liquor Store location on 4th Street in Los Ranchos de Albuquerque. They built the 19,000 square foot Village Shops at Los Ranchos and re-opened the Calico Café complete with outdoor seating, a bakery, a liquor store, and the high-scale Vernon's Hidden Valley Steakhouse.

Warning: when you step into the café, you will be confronted by a display case full of luscious cakes, cookies, and rolls. Take a look and decide if you need to save room for one of these before you leave.

When you are seated, make sure to order the house coffee, a blend made especially for the Calico Café. Deep, rich and eye-opening, this coffee is the way to start the day. Add to that the Calico French toast served with warm homemade peach brandy syrup and a side of breakfast pork or turkey bacon and you'll be ready for a full day on the range. Or maybe start with an omelet with spinach, cheese, and piñon nuts—definitely a tasty treat.

There are so many choices of eggs, New Mexican foods, potatoes, biscuits and grits to keep you going through all of your tasks during the day that you'll be on your second cup of coffee before you are ready to order. Although the breakfast menu items are only available until 2pm, breakfast burritos and breakfast quesadillas can be ordered all day.

Recommended Reading: Read the stories told by genuine cowgirls and cowboys in *Hot Biscuits: Eighteen Stories by Women and Men of the Ranching West* edited by Max Evans and Candy Moulton.

After Breakfast: Enjoy Albuquerque's natural beauty with a visit to the Rio Grande Nature Center. Start your visit off with a walk through the center learning about the plants and animals that are native to the *bosque*. Then continue your day by exiting through the back of the Nature Center and hiking through the *bosque* along the river trails.
www.rgnc.org

Church Street Café

2111 Church Street Northwest
Albuquerque, NM 87104
(505) 247-8522
www.churchstreetcafe.com

Breakfast Hours: Monday-
Saturday 8am-9pm,
Sunday 8am-4pm
Available all the hours the Café
is open. The exception is pancakes,
which are served only until noon
Kid Component:**
Prices: $$

Church Street Café is located in the Old Town area of Albuquerque, directly north of the San Felipe de Neri Church and the Old Town Plaza. Marie Coleman, owner, bought the property in 1994 and strived to keep the construction and décor authentic to early Albuquerque: some of the original wood floors and *vigas* (hand-hewn roof beams), were kept. The house was owned by the Ruiz family and was probably built around 1709. In its early years, it was an 18-room hacienda.

According to local legend, the last owner of the house, Sara Ruiz, haunts the dwelling. Sara was a *curandera*, or healer, who was likely held in high regard in her community during her lifetime. People who have had encounters with Sara's ghost have seen her sweeping, feeding unseen chickens, or moving items in the house.

Today, the Ruiz house is a long building with several dining rooms and a patio in the back. The enclosed patio has a water fountain with a pond in one corner. It is popular during the summer, especially for Sunday morning brunch. While the bubbling water fountain adds to the cool feel of the patio area, different types of native and non-native plants and trees shade the patio from the summer heat. Inside the café, the walls are decorated with Navajo blankets, and other arts and crafts made by local Hispanic and Native American artists. The café's lobby has a small store with a good selection of Southwestern Native American arts and crafts.

Church Street Café is well-known for its *carne adovada* (chunks of pork meat marinated in red chile and then slow cooked) which is delicious with eggs. For a treat, nothing beats a warm *sopapilla*: deep-fried bread smothered in honey.

Recommended Reading: A great book set in Albuquerque is *The Brave Cowboy* by Edward Abbey. Originally published in 1956, it was made into a movie in 1962 and starred Kirk Douglas. The movie, *Lonely Are the Brave*, is a must see as it includes scenes of Albuquerque and the Sandia Mountains in the late 1950s. This book reflects a change in attitude and laments the passing of the cowboy lifestyle. For a good short history of early Albuquerque, read Marc Simmons' *Hispanic Albuquerque*.

After Breakfast: *Way* after breakfast (when the sun has gone down), take an after-dark ghost tour to learn about the Church Street Café's "Sara" and more than a dozen other paranormal personalities who apparently (or not) have made Old Town their eternal home.
www.toursofoldtown.com

Cocina de Manuel

111 Coors Blvd. NW
Albuquerque, NM 87121
(505) 831-4435

Breakfast Hours:
Tuesday-Saturday 7am-3pm,
Sunday 8am-2pm
Kid Component:**
Prices: $

Cocina de Manuel is owned by Manuel and Lillian Ortega. Manuel is the chief cook while Lillian waits tables. Located on the northwest side of Albuquerque at Central and Coors NW, the restaurant blends into the strip mall where it's situated. Don't let this nondescript location fool you. Regulars are greeted by name and orders for "the usual" are the norm because Manuel's is the location for the best smothered breakfast burrito in the city, if not the state.

This is a burrito that hangs over the edges of the plate. Wrapped in a flour tortilla it is a combination of eggs, potatoes, and your choice of bacon or sausage, all smothered in red or green chile. It's a meal that will fill you up for the day, leaving you nearly uninterested in eating lunch or dinner. Try Manuel's version of Christmas—a ladleful of red chile inside the tortilla with green chile smothering the outside. It's good enough to come direct from Santa!

Breakfast, served all day, is not limited to the burrito. The *huevos rancheros* dish served with potatoes or rice is a real crowd pleaser. And the home fries are a favorite at any time of day.

Recommended Reading: Annie Collins Morgan, the title character in *Annie's Song* by Sabra Brown Steinsiek, is a Broadway actress with Albuquerque ties. Her roommate is an aspiring writer…an aspiring male writer. Their relationship is strictly platonic or, at least that's the plan. When Annie returns to Albuquerque to perform at the historic KiMo Theatre, her first stop is at Cocina de Manuel for green chile chicken enchiladas and sopapillas. When tragedy strikes back in New York City, it takes the ghost of the KiMo Theatre to help set it right.

After Breakfast: Spend a morning at the Rio Grande Zoo, since some animals are quite active at this time of day. Albuquerque's world-class zoo holds over 250 animal species.
www.cabq.gov/biopark/zoo

Christy Mae's

1400 San Pedro Dr. NE
Albuquerque, NM 87110
(505) 255-4740
www.christymaes.com

Breakfast Hours:
Monday-Saturday
7am-10:30am
Kid Component:***
Prices: $$

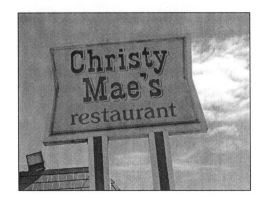

Christy Mae's is a family restaurant owned and operated by Larry Ashby and Joe, Jane, Andrew Tricario (the trio is pictured in the family portrait on the north wall of the restaurant). Located in Albuquerque's near northeast heights, just a few blocks north of the State Fairgrounds, Christy Mae's offers traditional country cooking with New Mexico flair. Cream gravy and green chile each have place of pride on the menu in a comfortable, country-cozy, watermelon-hued dining room. Farm implements, kitchen gadgets, old-fashioned ice cream ads, and the occasional roadrunner decorate the walls. The environment and the service are kid friendly, and the portions are generous.

After more than twenty years of serving meat and potatoes and soup and sandwiches for lunch and dinner, Christy Mae's began serving breakfast in 2007. It's a great place to meet friends, and the staff is happy to let you linger over your coffee and newspaper. The menu combines traditional eggs-and-bacon fare (if you're a gravy lover, try Colonel Ashby's SOS), breakfast burritos, *huevos rancheros*, and some of the restaurant's most popular sandwich choices, including the Albuquerque Turkey.

The coffee is always hot, fresh, and bottomless. If you like your coffee mug, you are welcome to buy one. If you're not a coffee drinker, try the cinnamon-orange spice tea. It's a sweet and refreshing way to start the morning.

Recommended Reading: *The Best Novels and Short Stories of Eugene Manlove Rhodes*, by Eugene Manlove Rhodes, edited by Frank V. Dearing. Two of our favorite stories in this collection are "Trusty Knaves" and "Pasó por Aquí." Rhodes's preference for outlaws over in-laws is clear in these works, and his rogues and heroes are fascinating, frequently charming, and committed to getting the job done.

After Breakfast: Take a trip up to the top of the Sandia Mountains via the Sandia Peak Tramway. On the tram, you will travel nearly three miles. Once reaching Sandia Peak, venture out on some of the walking trails for fresh air and stunning views.
www.sandiapeak.com

The Daily Grind

414 Central Ave. SE
Albuquerque NM 87102
(505) 883-8310
www.dailygrindunwind.com

Breakfast Hours:
Monday-Friday 7am-4pm,
Saturday 7:30am-4pm,
Sunday 9am-3pm
Kid Component:*
Prices: $$

"Charming" is an adjective not often applied to Albuquerque. The Daily Grind is a café deli whose charms include an eclectic décor, an historic setting, and a small but tasty menu of coffees, teas, baked goods, soups, salads, sandwiches and breakfasts.

The Daily Grind began as a family business in 1997 by Nancy and Mike Rogers, originally located at San Pedro and Candelaria NE. When they lost their lease in 2006, they decided to migrate to the Huning-Highlands neighborhood east of downtown. The Rogers renovated part of a duplex that formerly housed "La Patisserie" (a custom bakery), and Tom Davies' Used Bookstore in the 1980s. The Huning Highlands (1880) was the first residential subdivision in New Albuquerque, where Victorian mansions, cottages, railroad flats, and tuberculosis sanatoriums intermingled with local businesses along "Railroad Avenue."

The building housing The Daily Grind is part of a compound with a tree-shaded brick interior courtyard called Plaza Escalante. There have been small businesses in the compound since the 1920s, including a wedding chapel, portrait photographers, a dance studio, art galleries, software developers, and a letterpress printer. The east end of the compound houses the elegant Artichoke Café, one of Albuquerque's premiere restaurants. For forty years, the other half of the duplex was home to the Camera Shop of New Mexico.

Early morning breakfasts at this restaurant give diners a front row seat to watch Albuquerque culture and history on display. Central

Avenue is a constant parade of pedestrians, bikers, busses, cars and trucks traveling old Route 66. Across the street, the restored Albuquerque High School campus buildings and newly-built loft apartments house hundreds of new-urbanists, marking a victory for preservationist neighbors working to revive a declining area.

Customers can dine at tables in the courtyard, in a covered breezeway leading to Central, at sidewalk tables, or in the two glassed-in showrooms in the front part of the duplex.

The basic breakfast is an omelet made fresh with cheese, tomato, and green chile. You might also get the omelet as a breakfast special, with onion-y potatoes and a muffin; or in a flour tortilla breakfast burrito including beans, or on a bagel.

Waffles and French toast are available. The Daily Grind is properly famous for their buttery scones; raspberry and blueberry are made daily and other flavors are offered. Espresso and latte drinks are available along with coffee and teas. Salads feature fresh greens topped with walnuts, cranberries, and raspberry vinaigrette. Take-out is available, but leisurely dining with friends and colleagues sitting in the front window or the patio is a treat not to be missed.

Recommended Reading: To learn more about Albuquerque's historic neighborhoods, read *Historic Albuquerque Today* by Susan DeWitt. This illustrated survey of over 300 historic buildings tells the story of Albuquerque's establishment and growth, organized by neighborhoods. It covers the original Villa (Old Town), Rio Grande Valley Spanish farm villages, and the creation of New Town (downtown) with the arrival of the Santa Fe Railroad and the development of residential neighborhoods around New Town. Important residential, commercial, and institutional buildings are described in detail.

After Breakfast: A highlight in this neighborhood is the Special Collections Library across the street from The Daily Grind. One of 17 branches of the Albuquerque/Bernalillo County Library System, it is housed in the 1925 Pueblo-Spanish Revival style Old Main Library. The library features comprehensive local history and genealogy collections, and has a unique hands-on museum of the history of writing, books and printing: the Center for the Book. www.cabq.gov/library/specol.html

El Camino Dining Room

6800 4th St. NW
Los Ranchos de Albuquerque,
NM 87107
(505) 344-0448

Breakfast Hours:
Tuesday-Friday 7am-2:30pm,
Saturday & Sunday 7am-2pm
Kid Component:***
Prices: $

In 1950, Clyde Tyler built the El Camino Dining Room on 4th Street across from the El Camino Motor Lodge. The restaurant and motel have retained their original look and with only a few cosmetic changes here and there. If you want to experience the 50s, just sit at one of the front windows and look across the street or around the room. Neither place is fancy nor glamorous, but you get the true feeling of the 1950s.

The restaurant is open for breakfast and lunch all day. Order a green chile cheeseburger for breakfast, order pancakes for lunch, or have the *huevos rancheros* anytime! True New Mexico comfort food is served here. We recommend the "home fries," thick slabs of skillet-fried potatoes. Nothing is overly spicy, but everything has flavor.

You are in Los Ranchos de Albuquerque, settled about 1750 and incorporated in 1956. This is an agricultural area, full of people who still grow alfalfa and have livestock next to their houses. Many of the people who come in are regulars, and they know the owners, the cooks, and waitresses by name. Chances are, if your waitress isn't one of the owners, she is related to them. If you want information about something—not just the food, ask your waitress. These waitresses are as scrappy as the most tenacious librarians—if they don't know the answer to your question, they can probably find someone in the dining room who does. Take your time at this restaurant, look around, and relax. You aren't in Albuquerque any more. Eat, read and realize that you are in a neighborhood time warp.

Recommended Reading: If you tire of people-watching at the El Camino Dining Room, and you are curious about the "Route 66 pre-1937" signs along 4th Street, open *Route 66 Adventure Handbook: Updated and Expanded Third Edition* by Drew Knowles. This book includes all the old Route 66 alignments and where to find them now. It contains fascinating facts, suggestions of places to visit, and a heart-felt feeling of love for the old highway.

After Breakfast: Explore more of Albuquerque's historic Route 66 by visiting the Nob Hill area on Central Avenue. Several Route 66 landmarks still exist in this area of town. Shopping, watching people, and enjoying lunch are all recommended while visiting the historic Nob Hill area. www.rt66central.com

Flying Star

Acequia de Corrales
10700 Corrales Road
Albuquerque, NM 87114
(505) 938-4717
www.flyingstarcafe.com

Breakfast Hours:
Sunday-Thursday 6am-11pm,
Friday-Saturday 6am-11:30pm
Kid Component:***
Prices: $$

With their glass light fixtures, huge picture windows, and local artwork on display, Flying Star Cafés are a treat for the eyes as well as the stomach. But while their décor may draw new patrons inside, the food keeps them coming back.

These classy, funky joints are always hopping, sometimes to the point of making customers project evil thoughts onto other guests so they can score an empty table. Fortunately, the food ordering and delivery procedure is such that by the time you place your order and get your tray and drinks, a space often opens up. In warm weather the crowd spills out onto the friendly patios, where it's all too tempting to linger for an hour or more. The patios are dog friendly and referred to as "petios," so there is no doubt our four legged friends are invited to breakfast. Flying Star even sells special treats for Rex and Fido.

Breakfast is as grand or as minimal as you would like. Try the from-scratch, organic oatmeal topped with fruit and nuts, or New Mexico standards such as *huevos rancheros* and breakfast burritos, which come either smothered or as an easy-to-hold Graburrito. One of our favorite breakfast dishes is the Fiesta Morning, a Fiesta Roll (green chile cheese roll) split and filled with scrambled eggs, more cheese, and more green chile. You can always count on the chile to have a nice kick to it. Another specialty is the Southwest Bennie, a New Mexican version of eggs Benedict, with green chile in both the turkey sausage and the cheese sauce. Breakfast items are available all day, unless they are sold out.

Lighter appetites will gravitate toward the fresh baked goods, such as *pain au chocolat*, croissants, Danish and bagels. Flying Star also offers a generously proportioned bagel-and-lox combo that is a superb complement to coffee and the Sunday paper.

Many of the ingredients used at Flying Stars are organic. The eggs are from cage-free, vegetarian-fed, drug-free chickens. The bacon is applewood-smoked, and the green chile sausage comes from free-range turkeys.

At the time of this writing, there are nine Flying Star locations uniquely designed. While it is possible to order a light snack and eat relatively affordably, somehow we never manage to get out without spending twenty or thirty dollars. The offerings are so plentiful and inviting that we always end up taking home a little something for later— perhaps a piece of Key lime pie or an iced sugar cookie.

Other Locations

723 Silver Ave SW, Albuquerque, NM 87102 (505) 244-8099
4026 Rio Grande NW, Albuquerque, NM 87107 (505) 344-6714
8001 Menaul NE, Albuquerque, NM 87110 (505) 293-6911
4501 Juan Tabo NE, Albuquerque, NM 87111 (505) 275-8311
3416 Central SE, Albuquerque, NM 87106 (505) 255-6633
8000 Paseo Del Norte, Albuquerque, NM 87122 (505) 923-4211
200 South Camino del Pueblo, Bernalillo, NM 87004 (505) 404-2100
500 Market Street, Suite 1-L, Santa Fe, NM 87501

Recommended Reading: Corrales author Lisa Lenard-Cook interweaves the lives of several residents of the fictional town of Valle Bosque (which is modeled on Corrales) in *Coyote Morning*, a tale of humans vs. nature and suburb vs. country. Lenard-Cook successfully captures the age-old conflicts between old-timers and newcomers, a story told time and time again in many of New Mexico's small towns.

After Breakfast: If you have enjoyed your breakfast at the Corrales location, head to Casa San Ysidro, an historic home built by the Gutiérrez family in the 1870s.
www.cabq.gov/museum/history/casatour.html

Frontier Restaurant

2400 Central Ave SE
Albuquerque, NM 87106
(505) 266-0550

Breakfast Hours:
Daily 5am-1am
Kid Component:**
Prices: $

There are a lot of similarities between the Frontier Restaurant and Disneyland. Both are generally filled with throngs of people. Both have helpful signs to let you gauge your progress towards the order counter: "Approx. 10-minute wait from this point." Both sell souvenirs (t-shirts and mugs—okay, maybe Disneyland offers a few more souvenirs). Both have "lands" with specific themes. Technically, the Frontier is all "Frontier Land," but within it there is the John Wayne area, the Indian Rugs on the Ceiling area...you get the idea.

Many people have their favorite room at Frontier, and sometimes even their favorite booth or table, and it all depends on the décor. Some prefer the front room with the metal Lobo (University of New Mexico Mascot) sculpture by the entrance, wagon-wheel chandeliers, flat screen TV, and the bustle of the order counter and kitchen. Others become particularly fond of a certain painting, and insist on sitting at a table where they can gaze at that masterpiece throughout their meal. One fanatic, who shall remain nameless, always makes a beeline for the farthest east room (the one closest to the Sandias) because it houses what must be the world's largest painting of Elvis on velvet. If all the tables in that room are filled, she threatens to check into Heartbreak Hotel.

The art throughout the restaurant is great, but everyone really flocks to Frontier for the food. Due to the location on Central Avenue right across from the University of New Mexico, customers include

UNM students, faculty, and staff, in addition to Albuquerque residents and tourists. Everyone follows the same drill: come in, get in line, and peruse the menus mounted over multiple order stations. Gals with bandana head scarves or guys with Frontier/Golden Pride paper hats punch your selections into their registers, take your money, and hand you your drink choices on a tray along with the receipt containing your number. Find a table and start watching for your number to come up on the electronic boards mounted throughout the establishment. At the pickup counter, be sure and take time to marvel at the incredible tortilla machine, turning out hot fresh flour tortillas right before your eyes! (In the old days, this would have been worth an "E" ticket at Disneyland, even though you can't ride on it.)

Breakfast is available all day, and you will see students chowing down on pancakes during late-night study sessions, families mixing and matching burritos, *huevos rancheros*, and omelets for Sunday after-church brunch, and everyone else enjoying good food and plenty of it. The fabled Frontier Sweet Roll, almost too big for one person but share-able in a pinch, is required eating here. Served hot, this soft spiral filled with cinnamon and dripping with melted butter is scrumptious.

Recommended Reading: Key scenes in Tony Hillerman's *Coyote Waits* take place in the Frontier Restaurant. The descriptions are so vivid you can almost smell the Frontier rolls and hear the clanking of the tortilla machine. Recommended Viewing: You'll stroll into the Frontier and walk all the way back to the Velvet Elvis room with Detective Joe Leaphorn (played by actor Wes Studi) when you watch the video version of *Coyote Waits* produced for the PBS Mystery series by Robert Redford and Rebecca Eaton.

After Breakfast: Visit the University of New Mexico campus right across the street from the Frontier. One of our favorite stops is the UNM Bookstore. Zimmerman Library is located in the center of campus and is housed in a building of historic significance, designed by architect John Gaw Meem. www.unm.edu

Garcia's Kitchen

1113 4th St. NW
Albuquerque, NM 87102
(505) 247-9149
www.garciaskitchen.com

Breakfast Hours:
Monday-Saturday 6:30am-3pm,
Sunday 6:30am-2pm
Kid Component:**
Prices: $

When you walk through the door of the Original Garcia's Kitchen in Downtown Albuquerque (the true original in a family of seven restaurants located throughout the city), the dancing image of founder, entrepreneur, and bon vivant Andy Garcia greets you with a lively smile. You might think that this merry visage portends a fiesta, which makes sense when you know that the Garcia family also owns a successful "tent and event" business. Once you've stepped through the door, your hunch is confirmed: you find you've entered a celebration that is all about neighbors, friends, family, and food.

Garcia's Kitchen is a quintessentially local spot. Framed articles and awards randomly dotting the walls are testament to much public recognition. But the restaurant group is not without fame beyond the city limits. Recipes and the preparation of *carne adovada* and a *chorizo* breakfast burrito were featured on the Food Network show "FoodNation with Bobby Flay" (Albuquerque episode, BF1C14). Following a trip to the metro area by then-President Bill Clinton, Garcia's provisioned the departing Air Force One contingent with the savory and spicy local fare of green chile chicken enchiladas.

Chile is at the core of just about any breakfast entrée on the menu. The chile *rojo* is unfailingly fresh. With a slight orange tinge, it's a smooth and deeply flavored sauce that re-animates life from dried brittle pods. Chile *verde's* color is a deep, dark green. The *verde* is saucy in a different way from the *rojo,* strips and diced pieces of peppery, green flesh that are tangy with heat, awash in broth.

Menu choices combine chile with eggs in a variety of ways. As an alternative to omelets and *huevos rancheros*, try *huevos ala Mexicana* (finely diced jalapeños, onions, and tomatoes which can come "locos" by adding ham or beef). The breakfast burrito plate is meal enough for two (a thick tortilla filled with freshly scrambled eggs, crisp-chewy bacon, and *papas* all smothered with chile). *Carne adovada* (tender chunks of pork marinated in and sauced with red chile) and *chorizo* are savory specialties worth coming back for again and again, and *carnitas* (beef strips stewed in green chile) add spicy protein to standard breakfast fare. *Chicharrones* (deep-fried pork skin) and *menudo* (beef tripe served in broth) delight the true believers and hardcore palates.

"Gringo Breakfast" options pair eggs with steak, pork chops, ham, sausage or bacon (no chile). Pancakes, French toast, and Belgian waffles keep things sweet.

Hot entrées are served with creamy refried beans and pan-fried *papas*. Homemade tortillas, s*opapillas,* and toast are also available as accompaniments.

Other locations:

8515 Indian School NE, Albuquerque, NM 87110 (505) 292-5505
3601 Juan Tabo NE, Albuquerque, NM 87111 (505) 275-5812
1736 Central SW, Albuquerque, NM 87104 (505) 842-0273
4917 4th Street NW, Albuquerque, NM 87107 (505) 341-4594
2924 San Mateo NE, Albuquerque, NM 87123 (505) 888-3488
6961 Taylor Ranch NW, Albuquerque, NM 87120 (505) 899-7960

Recommended Reading: *Historic Albuquerque: An Illustrated History* by Carleen Lazzell and Melissa Payne is a book commissioned by the Albuquerque Conservation Association to commemorate the city's Tricentennial. This work provides an engaging context for your explorations of historic Albuquerque and extensive photos from the Albuquerque Museum archive and private sources augment this text.

After Breakfast: If you are dining at the 4th Street location, keep with the neighborhood spirit and explore the surrounding areas. We recommend walking south and venturing into Albuquerque's downtown.

Greenside Café

12165 North Hwy. 14
Cedar Crest NM 87008
(505) 286-2684
www.greensidecafe.net

Breakfast Hours:
Monday-Friday 11am-3pm,
Saturday-Sunday 8am-3pm
Kid Component:***
Prices: $$

Remember what happens in the song "The Bear Went Over the Mountain?" The bear goes over the mountain to see what he could see. But all that he could see...was the other side of the mountain! Hardly seems worth the trip, does it?

Well, if this were an Albuquerque bear, and he happened to go over the mountain (in this case the Sandia mountains) via I-40, traversed Tijeras Pass, and took the Cedar Crest exit, the trip would definitely be worthwhile—especially if he ended up at the Greenside Café.

Opened in the fall of 2007, this charming eatery's sunflower yellow, burgundy/brown or clear glass walls enclose several distinct eating areas. From four small bar-type round tables with barstools you can glimpse the kitchen, watch the servers, or look over to the hilltops covered with evergreens. The pleasant outdoor deck area features planters with an interesting assortment of grasses and blooming flowers in season. Other seating arrangements afford views of walls featuring art by local artists. One colorful grouping of oil paintings seemed so vibrant and alive you could almost smell the fresh paint. It was hard to resist touching them to see if they were still wet.

Greenside owner Jay Wulf was recently featured as a top chef to watch in *Albuquerque the Magazine*. He has been a partner, owner, and/or chef in several acclaimed Albuquerque restaurants. According to framed articles from area publications, Jay has also worked as a juggler, motorcycle mechanic, and ski instructor.

If at this point you're as hungry as a bear, it's time to consider the menu. Wulf's "soon to be famous" Sandia Toast is the basis for all things yummy! As much soufflé as traditional French toast, this dish is made with French bread and a little orange zest. It's fabulous with warm maple syrup and fresh fruit. Signature dishes such as the Hen Grenade (Sandia Toast, topped with ham and two poached eggs, smothered with hollandaise and served with red-skinned potatoes) owe it all to Sandia Toast. Classic breakfast burritos, *huevos rancheros*, and *chilaquiles* (tomato-soaked tortilla chips topped with two eggs your way, red or green chile and cheese, served with red-skinned potatoes and your choice of 'bacony' pinto beans or vegetarian black beans) will fill you up and satisfy your craving for a New Mexico breakfast.

Not quite so hungry? Try ordering "Just Breakfast" with two eggs, potatoes and either ham, sausage, bacon, or *carne*. In addition, there are plenty of creative vegetarian breakfast options. Daily specials are written in bright chalk on slate behind and above the counter where you place your order. Dessert specials have their own slate. "Jaymade" ice creams, handmade by Jay, sound delicious, and a person might be tempted to try mango sorbet as a fun breakfast treat.

Don't be surprised if Jay himself steps out of the kitchen to visit your table, make sure you are enjoying your meal, and remind you of the café's motto: "It always tastes better on the green side of the mountain."

Recommended Reading: Author Lois Duncan lived in Albuquerque for several years and many of her novels for young adults are set here. *Killing Mr. Griffin* is a chilling story with action taking place at Del Norte High School and in "a secluded area of the Sandias."

After Breakfast: Drive up to Sandia Crest and marvel at all the communications towers (they don't look this big from below!) Take in the panoramic view which, along with the altitude, almost takes your breath away. You'll be at an elevation of 10,678 feet, the highpoint on the Turquoise Trail National Scenic Byway.
www.turquoisetrail.org

Java Joe's

906 Park Avenue SW
Albuquerque, NM 87102
(505) 765-1514
www.downtownjavajoes.
com

Breakfast Hours:
Daily 6:30am-3:30pm
Kid Component:*
Prices: $

When you step in to Java Joe's, you step into a little of East Village, New York, just off Central Avenue in Albuquerque. First there are the yellow and red walls, then the changing artwork from kitchen cabinet doors painted with saints, to postcards of classic Route 66 neon signs marking motels and steak houses. You may even find a two-piece ensemble playing folk and rock tunes.

Southwest fare ranges from black bean burritos to *huevos rancheros* to breakfast enchiladas to tofu burritos to the enticing Turquoise Trail Omelet of sautéed mushrooms, bacon, avocado, and Swiss cheese. Pancakes include buttermilk, strawberries and cream, and blueberry granola. On the healthy side there's a fruit yogurt parfait or a braised tofu/vegetable scramble with toast. Or, go with the NYC theme and have a great plate of lox and bagel, with cream cheese, capers, tomatoes, onions, olives, and lettuce. Vegetarian fare is plentiful.

Looking around the restaurant, you will notice patrons seem to from the local neighborhood and Albuquerque's downtown government and businesses. The eclectic crowd from business professionals to artists to college students exhibit dress styles ranging from suit and tie to t-shirt to body art.

Recommended Reading: While walking around downtown, you may find yourself interested in *Albuquerque Downtown: From a Geologic Point of View—A Walking Tour of the City Center* by George S. Austin. This three mile walking tour of downtown will point out the historic architecture and materials used to construct Albuquerque's downtown buildings.

After Breakfast: Built in 1927 as a vaudeville theatre and movie palace, The KiMo Theatre is a treasured Albuquerque landmark hosting live performances in a historic venue. Located at 5th and Central NW, the renovated KiMo features elaborate Native American ornamentation in the Pueblo Deco architectural style. Also explore Albuquerque's Main Library, located at 5th and Copper. It is within walking distance of the KiMo Theatre and Java Joe's.
www.cabq.gov/kimo

Jimmy's Café on Jefferson

7007 Jefferson NE
Albuquerque, NM 87109
(505) 341-2546

Breakfast Hours:
Monday-Friday 6:30am-2:30pm
Saturday-Sunday 7am-2pm
Kid Component:***
Price: $$

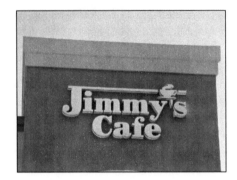

When Steve Reynolds opened this restaurant in 2003 he wanted to call it "Steve's" and decorate it with pictures of famous people named Steve. But when he couldn't think of very many famous Steves, he decided to call it "Jimmy's" after his son. There are plenty of folks with *that* name, or derivations thereof, including presidents, kings, saints, performers, singers, and sports figures, not to mention a particularly famous cricket from a beloved Disney movie. The walls are covered with pictures and photos of them!

Steve did manage to get his own name on the menu, however, with "Steve's Breakfast": a pile of hash browns covered with red or green chile, topped with two eggs any style, with jack and cheddar cheeses.

There are almost as many breakfast choices as there are Jims, James, Jamies, and Jimmys on the walls. Many entrées come with hash browns or fresh fruit and choice of toast or tortilla. The breakfast quesadilla is a dilly, and the *carne adovada*, which can turn up in everything from enchiladas to omelets to skillets is sublime. Hotcakes, plain or with additional pecans, blueberries, chocolate chips, or strawberries come in tall (4) or short (2) stacks. If your appetite is huge, tackle the "Pork n' Produce Omelet" which features ham, bacon, sausage, *carne adovada*, onions, bell peppers, mushrooms, red or green chile, and a topping of cheddar and jack cheeses. The burritos at Jimmy's are spectacular, each containing three scrambled eggs and assorted fillings. For a small extra charge, burritos can be made with a chipotle or spinach tortilla. Note to environmentalists and food lovers: it's a real treat to go "green" with that spinach tortilla. And then there's the pizza. Who ever heard of pizza for breakfast? Jimmy's has. Ten varieties are available with an "additional toppings" list of 20 items.

A Happy Face Pancake with chocolate chips and whipped topping is just one of the offerings on the Kids portion of the menu. Children can also scarf down five Silver Dollar Pancakes while figuring out why Kermit the Frog appears on the huge wall mural. (Hint: he is shown with his creator, Jim Henson.)

You won't have to wish upon a star for help in identifying the 100+ famous Jimmys whose likenesses adorn the walls. Just ask your server if you can view the "List of Jimmys."

Recommended Reading: Any of poet Jimmy Santiago Baca's collections are definitely food for thought. Look for his *Winter Poems Along the Rio Grande* or *Martín & Meditations on the South Valley.*

After Breakfast: Visit the Anderson Abruzzo International Balloon Museum where you will learn about the history and science behind Albuquerque's biggest annual international event.
www.balloonmuseum.com

The Range Café and Bakery

925 S. Camino Del Pueblo
Bernalillo NM 87004
(505) 867-1700
www.rançecafe.com

**Breakfast Hours: Daily
7:30am-3pm
Kid Component:***
Price: $$**

The Range Café is easily an institution of Albuquerque cuisine. There are three locations, two in Albuquerque and the original in Bernalillo. All three serve a fine menu of great southwestern dishes for lunch and dinner with plenty of New Mexican flair, but it is undoubtedly the breakfast menu that has made The Range Café famous. There's something for everyone, from the basic eggs and bacon appetite to the more adventurous green-chile-on-everything kind of eater. The atmosphere in each individual Range Café is playful and pleasant, sporting unique southwestern artwork, and memorabilia galore.

While you can get a great dining experience at any of the three locations around town, it's the original Range Café and Bakery in Bernalillo that makes for a real adventure in dining, literally, due to its somewhat out of the way location. From Albuquerque, head north up the old Scenic Route 66 all the way to Bernalillo. Along the way, you'll enjoy a beautiful view of the Sandia Mountains. From Santa Fe, just hit I-25 and head south to the Bernalillo exit, and west to Scenic Route 66 south. Both ways are truly pleasant and breathtakingly beautiful little drives with a fantastic prize at the end: good eats, and plenty of 'em!

The funky décor, the rustic furniture, and the great service are reason enough to visit The Range, but the food is the jewel in the sombrero. The award winning *huevos rancheros* is the dish to get if you aren't from around here, and you are looking for that special something that tells you you're eating the right stuff. This entrée comes complete with eggs however you want them, beans, blue corn tortillas filled with cheese, and plenty of fresh fixings on the side, like plump tomatoes and crisp lettuce. If you want to guarantee a good late morning nap, then you'll want to fill up on the Wagon Train (two eggs, two slices of bacon, two sausages, two pancakes, chopped grilled potatoes, and beans). There is a good selection of vegetarian options as well.

For an unbelievably sweet experience, try the stuffed French toast, thick slices of homemade cinnamon toast bursting with bananas and strawberries, and covered with homemade apple butter.

The kids get a special menu that includes some unique drinks such as "Life by Soda" that is a mix of just about every kind of soda you can think of. The Four Bit Cakes (four kid-sized silver dollar pancakes) are a real hit with at least one little girl we know, but the menu has all the good stuff a kid could want to eat and a parent could want to feed them. Be sure to look for the collection of toy ranges (stoves) on display in each location. There are no Easy-Bake Ovens here.

Other locations:
4401 Wyoming Blvd. NE, Albuquerque, NM 87111 (505) 293-6633
2200 Menaul Blvd. NE, Albuquerque, NM 87107 (505) 888-1600

Recommended Reading: Judith Van Gieson's mystery, Land of Burning Heat, is set in Bernalillo. Recent research has revealed that a large number of Jewish families fleeing from the Inquisition moved to what is now New Mexico. Van Gieson's heroine, archivist Claire Reynier, delves into the deep secrets found in one of these families.

After Breakfast: If you have enjoyed breakfast at The Range's Bernalillo location, take a quick drive over to Coronado State Monument. Explore the ancient ruins of the Pueblo of Kuaua, and imagine what it might have been like when the Spanish Explorer arrived in this area with 300 soldiers and 800 Native Americans in search of the Seven Cities of Gold. www.nmmonuments.org/inst.php?inst=4

Satellite Coffee

1642 Alameda Road NW
Albuquerque, NM 87114
(505) 899-1001
www.satcoffee.com

Breakfast Hours: Hours of operation vary by store and can be found on the website.
Price: $
Kid Component:**

Satellite Coffee is a local franchise in Albuquerque. The five coffee shops, owned by Mark Bernstein (also owner of the Flying Star Café), can be found throughout the city and are a popular hangout for customers of all ages.

The Alameda store is particularly busy on the weekends. Customers standing in the morning line (which sometimes reaches out the front door) can browse the many coffee choices in the scoop-it-yourself and grind-it-yourself line-up of beans inside the door. After passing the beans, you can peruse the selection of bakery goods while you wait to make your order. A glass display case contains breakfast musts like croissants, scones, various bagels, and English muffins. A specialty is the Fiesta Green Chile Roll, which is sure to fulfill the craving of anyone in need of a green chile fix. For a special sweet treat, customers can choose the cheese Danish. This goodie is filled with a creamy, sweet, cheese mixture and is well-matched with a London Fog drink, described as Earl Grey tea with steamed milk and a shot of vanilla.

For those looking for a more hearty breakfast, the shop offers three special burritos to choose from: the Rise & Shine, Americana Graburrito, and the NM Graburrito. Descriptions of these burritos and the many lunch items that are offered can be found on four large black boards, framed in oak, which hang on the shop's wall behind the counter. All of the food on the menu is available until it runs out—and on a busy day, that might not take too long.

Morning coffee lovers will be pleased with the menu's drink choices. Customers can enjoy one of Satellite's many coffee flavors, or select from the wide array of tea leaves, stored in large glass jars on display behind the counter.

If you would like to add a little kick to your drink, a self-serve counter with cream, sugar, and other flavorings like cinnamon and mocha powder is available.

When you visit this café you can grab your orders and go, or you can choose to soak up the sights and sounds of the coffee shop.

Those ready to relax can take a seat on one of the couches or leather chairs, or if a "working-meal" is in order, Satellite also provides seating with small tables, just the right size for a laptop or two. The table in front of the fireplace has a chessboard painted on it for those who enjoy a challenge. Customers can surf the internet for free while they listen to the variety of music that is pumped through speakers throughout the shop, and ranges from jazz to eclectic tunes.

Satellite displays the work of local artists on its walls, and offers a variety of items for purchase, such as coffee cups, postcards, and other knick-knacks for collectors of everything coffee.

Other locations:
3513 Central NE, Albuquerque, NM 87106 (505) 256-0345
8405 Montgomery Blvd. NE, Albuquerque, NM 87111 (505) 296-7654
2201 Louisiana Blvd. NE, Albuquerque, NM 87110 (505) 884-0098
2300 Central SE, Albuquerque, NM 87104 (505) 254-3800

Recommended Reading: Explore restaurants and hotels with Marilee Levitay in Cathryn Alpert's fictional novel, *Rocket City*. Marilee travels to Alamogordo from California to surprise her fiancée, but meets folks along the way who make her question her decision to marry.

After Breakfast: Continue the theme of satellites and rockets and plan a visit to the National Atomic Museum to learn about nuclear science. The museum follows the history of nuclear technology from its birth in Los Alamos to its current peaceful uses.
www.atomicmuseum.com

Weck's

1620 Rio Rancho Blvd. SE
Rio Rancho, NM 87124
(505) 896-1411
www.wecksinc.com

Breakfast Hours:
Daily 6:30am-2pm
Kid Component:***
Prices: $$

Where can you eat when Mom wants some *huevos rancheros*, Dad's in the mood for an omelet, and the kids are looking for pancakes or cinnamon rolls? Weck's is the place that will satisfy everyone's breakfast needs.

Weck's is a diner in spirit, serving up tasty, made-from-scratch food and lots of it, without any faux-diner trappings. The Albuquerque area features eight Weck's, with the unusual name derived from the name of the original owner, Doug Weckerly.

Weck's boasts "full belly" portions with every serving, and they aren't kidding. The pancakes are about eight inches across and three-quarters of an inch thick, while the egg dishes practically spill off the plate and onto the table. Just order what you want and don't be afraid to ask for a to-go box.

The menu is quite varied, with a selection of New Mexican favorites like *carne adovada* breakfast burritos and *huevos rancheros*, as well as American classics such as French toast, biscuits and gravy, and for those who are really hungry, chicken fried steak and eggs. You can even order lunch fare like hamburgers for breakfast.

On one recent visit, we enjoyed the Olde Time Favorite Omelet— four eggs with red and green chile, stuffed with ham and topped with melted cheddar and jack cheese. Like many of the breakfast offerings it was served with hash browns and toast. The toast choices include raisin, wheat, sourdough, and English muffins. Both the red and green chile were flavorful, but the green was hotter. The hash browns are crunchy on the outside, soft and shredded inside.

Another one of our favorites is the *papas*, which is hash browns topped with red and/or green chile, eggs and cheese, served in a big bowl. The coffee is diner-quality, medium strength, and they have yet to let us empty a cup.

The décor is not fancy, tables and chairs are clean and serviceable, and the surroundings are enhanced by local artists' paintings on the walls.

The Rio Rancho Weck's lot is often filled with balloonists' trucks. Although we have never felt hurried when lingering at a table, weekend mornings can be busy. Groups will wait patiently to be seated, and you can bet many of those waiting are regulars. It's not unusual to hear a customer call a waitress "Hon" or to see one of the servers give a patron a hug. The manager usually comes around to check on your eating experience, too. Weck's is a friendly place and the ideal spot for a hearty, filling breakfast

Other locations:

3913 Louisiana NE, Albuquerque, NM 87110 (505)881-0019
2039 4th St. NW, Albuquerque, NM 87102 (505) 242-1226
4500 Osuna Rd NE, Suite 100, Albuquerque, NM 87109 (505) 344-1472
1105 Juan Tabo Blvd. NE, Albuquerque, NM 87112 (505) 293-3154
6311 Riverside Plaza Lane, Albuquerque, NM 87120 (505) 352-6209
933 San Mateo Blvd. NE, Suite 100, Albuquerque, NM 87108 (505) 265-9237
6650 Holly NE, Suite C4, Albuquerque, NM 87113 (505) 821-9816

Recommended Reading: While it may be difficult to find, *Rio Rancho: A History, 1961–1982,* by Shiela Jane Furstenberg provides an intriguing look at the early days of Rio Rancho. A more readily available title, *Albuquerque: The Next Boomtown* by Cheryl Seas Gorder, contains a chapter on Rio Rancho and puts its growth in context with the rest of the Albuquerque area.

After Breakfast: Visit the Petroglyph National Monument and spend some time at the visitor's center and on the hiking trails where you will have the opportunity to spot over 20,000 ancient rock-art drawings.
www.www.nps.gov/petr

The Main Street Bistro

122 N. Main Street
Aztec, NM 87410
(505) 334-0109
www.aztecmainstreetbistro.
com

Breakfast hours:
Monday-Friday 7am-2pm,
Saturday 8am-noon
Kid component:**
Price: $

Stop and enjoy a delightful breakfast at the Main Street Bistro in Aztec. The restaurant ambience invites its customers with bright colors, local artwork, local newspapers, and cheerful service. One of the best things about the Main Street Bistro is the expectation that when you enter the establishment you will discover something good. Tony's quiche is such a discovery. Quiche with bacon and green chile or artichoke combine with cheese to provide a satisfying taste experience.

At least one local librarian would not have made it through her master's degree in library science without the brain food that Tony's quiche provided. Each Saturday she would walk to the Bistro for breakfast; upon returning home she would knock out assignment after assignment fueled by nutritious food and excellent coffee.

Another one of our favorite selections is the flaky cinnamon roll. Tasting a Bistro cinnamon roll creates an experience full of mystery with cinnamon spices causing your taste buds to pop.

Breakfast at the Main Street Bistro with the rich aromas of

brewed coffee and the experience of tasting various culinary delights prompts your soul to sing with joy. You will not regret any effort to enjoy breakfast at The Main Street Bistro in Aztec.

Recommended Reading: *Mama Fela's Girls* by Ana Baca is the account of a 1930s Hispanic family. The book will engage your thoughts, make you smile, and generate memories of personal family trials and joys. It includes stories with kitchen and cooking scenes, all of which match the sense of joy and good food found at the Main Street Bistro.

After Breakfast: Plan to visit the Aztec National Monument. The Puebloan culture at this World Heritage Site includes a great kiva and 500 masonry rooms.
www.nps.gov/azru

Belen

Harla May's Fat Boy Grill

710 Dalies Avenue
Belen, NM 87002
(505) 864-2211
www.harlamays.com

Breakfast Hours:
Thursday – Saturday,
10:57am-9:57pm,
Sunday 8:57am-6:57pm
Kid Component:***
Price: \$\$

Have you ever dreamed of having a side order of Milk Duds along with your breakfast? Did you think that eating candy for breakfast was something that could only happen in the movies? Well hold on to your fedora, Indy—at Harla May's Fat Boy Grill your dream can come true!

The building itself is your first clue that you are in for a theatrical dining experience. Harla May's occupies the building that was once the historic Oñate movie theater, located a couple of blocks off Belen's main drag.

As you walk through the door, you'll find yourself in a theater lobby featuring an authentic snack bar complete with candy and soft drinks. As the hostess escorts you to your table, located inside the old theater, be prepared to be overwhelmed. The walls are covered with enough memorabilia to keep a movie buff or Belen historian occupied for weeks. Tables occupy the upper level, but downstairs are several rows of original movie seats and more tables. A high-tech sound and sight system enables the management to project movies and other video presentations on the theater screen. The restaurant stage also hosts live musical acts.

If you are looking for a place to grab a fast breakfast, you might think twice. We encourage you to allow extra time to look at all the fascinating stuff that owner Anthony Baca has attached to the walls, ceiling, and just about any other area not devoted to dining accommodations.

Speaking of dining, that's why you're here, right? The fun menu provides a wonderful variety of burritos, French toast, chicken fried steak, Belgian waffles, *huevos rancheros*, biscuits, hotcakes, breakfast slams, and sides. As you munch, imagine those thrilling days of yesteryear when Belen children came to the theater for Saturday matinees of Hopalong Cassidy cowboy movies, Flash Gordon space serials, and Daffy Duck cartoons.

At the time of this writing Harla May's is open Thursday through Sunday. When questioned about the unusual opening and closing times, owner Anthony Baca says "If I told you we opened at 11 (or 9 on Sundays) you might not remember. But 10:57 (8:57 on Sundays) sticks in your head!"

Recommended Reading: Set in 1919, *Harvey Girl* by Sheila Wood Foard is the story of fourteen-year-old Clara Fern Massie. After running away from her family's farm in Missouri to find adventure, Clara becomes a Harvey Girl, one of the waitresses who worked at Harvey House restaurants along the railroads in the Southwest United States.

After Breakfast: Follow the sound of modern day train whistles to the Harvey House Museum at 104 North 1st Street, right next to the railroad tracks.
www.nmculturaltreasures.org/cgi-bin/instview.cgi?_recordnum=HARV

Bloomfield

Roadside Restaurant

319 S. Bloomfield Blvd.
Bloomfield, NM 87413
(505) 632-9940

Breakfast Hours:
Daily 5am-11am
Kid Component:***
Prices: \$\$

The Roadside Restaurant sits near the intersection of the two main highways running through Bloomfield: Highway 550 (Bloomfield Boulevard) and Highway 64. From the outside, the diner looks like a chain restaurant that would be associated with a chain motel and it is indeed next to a motel. However, it is not a chain nor has it ever been. It is an independently owned and operated establishment. Employees have praised the owner for being a community-minded person who supports local groups, especially from the high school.

The parking lot is always crowded with pickup trucks (an excellent indication of a local favorite). Step inside and you will find the parking lot has not led you astray. Jeans-wearing workers and families alike are at the tables and in the booths. Their conversations stretch between tables and everyone seems to know the waitresses and each other. That doesn't mean you'll feel like an outsider, though.

The décor is very much that of a diner, but with a little twist. The restaurant displays a large collection of Coca Cola memorabilia. Old lunch boxes and toy Coca Cola trucks are especially fun. The permanent display of Coca Cola Christmas items is truly amazing with toy trains and Christmas bears. We can't imagine how the owner found all of this stuff! The collection is so impressive that people travel from all over the state to appreciate it.

The food could be described as down home and all orders come in generous portions. Typical American breakfasts of eggs and hot cakes are offered. The hash browns are a stand out; very crisp on the outside, just the way we think they should be. But that's not all that's on the menu. Biscuits are made from scratch in-house. You can get biscuits and gravy or you can skip the gravy and get a biscuit instead of toast with your eggs and hash browns. There are also very hearty breakfasts like steak and pork chops served with eggs. Chicken fried steak is one of the most popular breakfasts served.

Because Bloomfield is in New Mexico after all, the restaurant cannot get away without offering some good New Mexico options. Breakfast burritos, *huevos rancheros*, and even *carne adovada* round out this home cooking menu.

The restaurant has its loyal, daily customers. They are mostly men and some have been coming every day for the past 25 years. A couple of regulars order the same thing every single day: one orders oatmeal (it was mentioned by people we talked to more than once) and another orders eggs with a side of beans.

This is a place where the food is simple but done well and the waitresses call you "Honey" and mean it. Look for the daily specials.

Recommended Reading: Take a different kind of trip with *The Lightning Field: Travels in and Around New Mexico* by Robert Eaton. You will not find the usual travel book here. What you will find is New Mexico off the beaten path and stories of the people who call those places home. There are stunning insights into the landscape and the interactions of the characters drawn to them by a curious and patient man on the road to finding himself.

After Breakfast: Bloomfield is surrounded by unique natural features such as Bisti Wilderness Badlands to the south. Navajo Lake, a prime New Mexico boating and fishing area is located just 25 miles upstream on the San Juan River. The area is rich in archeological sites from Chaco Canyon to Salmon Ruins. It is near the Four Corners National Monument, a popular tourist destination, and the only place in the United States where four states meet.

Capitan

Smokey Bear Restaurant

310 Smokey Bear Blvd.
Capitan, NM 88315
(575) 354-2257

Breakfast Hours: Monday-
Sunday: 6am-11am
Kid Component:***
Prices: $

Smokey Bear Restaurant is a landmark in Capitan, NM. Located directly in the beautiful heart of historical Lincoln County, it is the original birthplace as well as the burial place of Smokey Bear. You can visit Smokey's grave at the Smokey Bear Museum in Capitan.

The restaurant is a family-oriented establishment owned and operated by Rhonda and Zach Malott. It has a lengthy history, having opened in the early 1960s. The Malotts have had the eatery since 2004. Since they have owned the restaurant, it has been painted, the roof repaired, the heating and cooling updated, and new chairs installed. It is not difficult to find as it is situated in the middle of town with a large carved bear adorning the parking lot.

Smokey Bear Restaurant is world famous, and has had movie scenes filmed within its walls. It has been the backdrop for taped interviews with historians, actors and other important people. Inside, you will find posters of Smokey Bear and the movie, *The Outfitters*.

Breakfast time is always busy and the restaurant can accommodate a large crowd with numerous tables, booths, and seating at the counter. The food is country fare. Eggs are served scrambled, fried or in omelets, along with bacon, sausage, ham, and hash brown or tater tots. (Our very favorite is the green chile omelet.) You also get a choice of toast or biscuits. There are several varieties of hot cakes and waffles available. There is a coffee group that meets each morning and the staff keep pots going just for them. The coffee is always fresh and refills are endless.

When you enter the restaurant, the staff greets you as if you are old friends. They are attentive and one seldom waits more than 15 minutes for a meal. When you read the menu prices, you will feel like you have stepped back in time. "*A fabulous meal at a fair price*" is the motto of Smokey Bear Restaurant.

Recommended Reading: Written for children and adults alike, *Hot Foot Teddy: The True Story of Smokey Bear* by Sue Houser contains the true history of Smokey Bear. A portion of the proceeds benefits the Smokey Bear Forest Fire Prevention Program. Photographs, illustrations, and antique images of Smokey Bear are included. A fire in Lincoln County ignites the action in *The Big Gamble*, Michael McGarrity's seventh Kevin Kerney Mystery.

After Breakfast: The Smokey Bear Historical Park is located on highway 380 (better known as 118 Smokey Bear Blvd.) in the heart of Capitan. Completed in 1979, the park was established to honor Capitan's favorite son, Smokey, the little bear cub that was found with burned paws after a 17,000 acre forest fire in 1950 in the nearby Capitan Mountains. Also plan a visit to the Capitan Public Library, a top-notch library run with an all-volunteer staff.
www.emnrd.state.nm.us/fd/SmokeyBear/SmokeyBearPark.htm
www.capitanlibrary.org

The Blue House Bakery and Café

609 N. Canyon Street
Carlsbad, NM 88220
(575) 628-0555

Breakfast Hours: Monday-Friday
6am-2pm, Saturday 6am-noon
Kid Component:***
Prices: $

The Blue House Bakery and Café is a unique gourmet coffee shop with both indoor and outdoor patio dining. This restaurant's primary charm is found in the fact that the café is really a gently-converted quaint little house—painted blue, of course! A trip to the Blue House makes you feel as if you've stopped by your best friend's place for a cup of coffee, a feeling which owner Ginny Gregory has cultivated for the last several years.

You'll feel anything but "blue" when you start your day with something delicious from the Blue House. Breakfast selections include a wide variety of pastries and baked goods. Spinach and feta cheese or ham and cheese croissants are a specialty.

Sweet treats include the fruit-filled croissants, sticky buns, and cinnamon rolls. Scones are baked fresh daily and come in many flavors, including walnut, lemon, piñon, raisin, cranberry-almond, and even orange with white chocolate (a Saturday morning favorite). The Morning Glory Muffin, which tastes a little bit like carrot cake, is very popular. The batter includes raisins, zucchini squash, and carrots. Seasonal muffins might include peach in the summertime and pumpkin in the fall.

You can choose from one of several hot breakfasts, including French toast with sausage, or a breakfast burrito. Homemade granola baked with oats, raisins, nuts, honey, and cranberries and served with your choice of milk and a fresh banana is also available.

The Blue House is the place to go if you're a lover of coffee beverages. In addition to regular coffee, the Blue House serves up a variety of hot and cold espresso drinks. For a breakfast drink full of vitamins, try the fresh carrot juice with a dash of ginger, or orange juice squeezed fresh on the premises. Maybe a smoothie sounds good? You have your choice of peach/strawberry or an all-berry smoothie, both of which contain no added sugar. Hot tea, Chai tea and hot chocolate (topped with whipped cream) are also available. If you plan to stay and chat with a friend for a while, order a bottomless cup of coffee with unlimited refills.

The Blue House bakes fresh bread daily, so if you'd like to buy a loaf to take home, you can choose from whole wheat, rye, country white, and French baguettes.

Blue House is kid-friendly, especially if you sit outside where your child can enjoy the porch swing or examine the flowerbeds for ladybugs and butterflies. A vine-covered fence surrounds the outdoor seating area, and a gnarled old mulberry tree overhanging some of the tables in the side yard makes for a rather magical setting to enjoy your morning muffin.

Recommended Reading: *Cavern*, a novel by New Mexico author Jake Page, is set in the Carlsbad area. Jack Whittaker has discovered a cave to rival Carlsbad Caverns, the national park visited by hundreds of thousands of tourists each year. He needs to keep it a secret until he can get the rights to develop it. There are other secrets nearby, too. Who made the ancient footprints in the cave? And what is causing disappearances in a man-made cavern nearby, where government employees are working to store nuclear waste underground? Does it have something to do with the ancient subterranean creature, whose existence no one suspects?

After Breakfast: Take an hour and a half drive southwest of Carlsbad and head to the Guadalupe Mountains where you can hike and enjoy magnificent landscapes or spend time learning about the people who have inhabited this area for over 10,000 years.

Calloway's Café

110 N. Halaçueno Street
Carlsbad, NM 88220
(575) 887-6820

Breakfast Hours:
Tuesday-Friday 6am-2pm,
Saturday 7am-noon
Kid Component:**
Prices: $

Have you ever wondered how many people you can fit into a two-room restaurant? Come to Calloway's Café and you'll find out!

As you enter the fire red glass-paneled country door, you are greeted by the tinkling of a cheery bell and a smile from the cashier. It's just like stepping back in time into a quaint 1950s diner. Many mornings you will be greeted warmly by owner Tammy Kilgore, who is lending a hand with a mega-watt smile and a quick "Hello, how are you today? Glad you came to see us!"

You will be led to your seat at a table covered with a bright red gingham check print and small galvanized steel buckets to keep the condiments at bay. You will feel as if you are right at home. The sizzling of bacon, the clanking of spatulas and the chattering of the cook staff is heard through the open kitchen.

Their cozy building (which previously housed both the first post office in Carlsbad and the credit union for Duval Potash Mine) is dedicated to the potash miners who are the backbone of the Carlsbad community. "Calloway's Café—Proudly Serving Carlsbad's Potash Miners" is prominently written across their façade.

Here you will find a mini mining museum including fascinating photographs of miners past and present, operation sites, logo stickers, product sacks, miner's belts, hard hats, core samples, roof bolts, and boots.

"Bring your appetite" is not just a saying; it's a warning when visiting Calloway's Café! The old-fashioned buttermilk pancakes are nearly one-inch thick and they lap over the edges of the ten-inch plate on which they are served. The enormous portions follow through to the entire menu including the Belt Crew Build Your Own Burritos. We're talking a five-inch girth on just one burrito! With these burritos, you choose the meats, cheeses, and veggies (avocado is an option). Every menu item will cause your eyes to bug at just the portion size alone; the taste will finish you off.

Any meat and egg breakfast is also served with your choice of hash brown or home fried potatoes and toast or biscuits and gravy. We don't know how Calloway's affords to serve these portions, but we're glad they do since no one goes away hungry.

Hint: Get there early for the best seating. Quarters are cramped, but well worth the wait.

While in Calloway's Café, take the time to read the Potash Miner's Prayer and A Miner's Worth proudly displayed on their walls. They'll bring a tear to your eye, but also make you glad you have supported an establishment dedicated to these hard working people.

Calloway's is located on Halagueno Street across from City Hall and only half a short block from the Carlsbad Public Library. You can't beat that location!

Recommended Reading: In keeping with the mining theme, the action packed mystery *The Man Who Killed Shakespeare* by Ken Hodgson lets you follow the trials, tribulations, and high hopes of the tiny gold mining town, Shakespeare, New Mexico in the post-depression era. Hodgson, a Tucumcari horse rancher, bases the majority of his books in the history-drenched boot heel section of New Mexico.

After Breakfast: Visit the Waste Isolation Pilot Plant (WIPP) Experience Exhibit at 4021 National Parks Highway for a virtual tour that takes you 2,150 feet underground into ancient salt deposits left by the Permian Sea before dinosaurs roamed the earth. Experience hands-on learning and take home a 250-million-year-old salt sample.
www.wipp.energy.gov

Happy's

4103 National Parks Hwy
Carlsbad, NM 88220
(575) 887-8489

Breakfast Hours: Monday-
Wednesday 5am-3pm,
Thursday-Saturday 5am-9pm
Kid Component:***
Prices: $

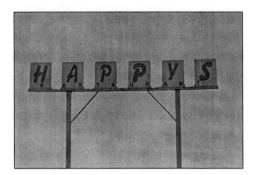

If you remember static-laden AM radios, AMC Pacers, or the oil embargo of the 1970s, you will recognize the shape of the Happy's building—it was a Stuckey's. Stuckey's, the original convenience store, was a welcome oasis aside the long Interstates and highways across the country. And who could forget Stuckey's Pecan Log Rolls? Travel along the National Parks Highway on the way to the Carlsbad Caverns and you will see the familiar building shape, only now the Stuckey's sign is replaced with a cheerful yellow and red Happy's sign.

Walking through the door, you enter into a world where happiness rules. Owner Carol Modrall has collected smiley face memorabilia for many years and is proud to display it everywhere in her restaurant. We couldn't help but feel cheerful while surrounded by so many smiley faces!

Happy's is a casual, old-fashioned dining experience. You will be just as comfortable whether dressed in tourist togs or a business suit. No matter the attire, everyone places their order at the front counter. One hint: if you want green chile on an item—tell them to make it an "olé." Your drink can be found at the drink fountain just a few steps from the order counter. After placing your order and filling your drink, settle into a comfortable booth, read the newspaper, and listen to the robust laugh of Happy's owner and her staff.

Be prepared to have a hearty meal. Happy's does not skimp on portions or quality. They proudly say they are the "Home of the Jumbo Breakfast," and they mean it! The Jumbo Two-Egger is two extra large AA eggs, a mound of country spuds, toast, and your choice of thick bacon, sausage, or ham. This is a big breakfast, but there's a bigger breakfast than that! The Extra-Jumbo Three-Egger comes with the same choices, but with one more egg. These entrées can be translated into a burrito if you prefer. The green chile omelet is huge and filled to the brim with delicious New Mexico green chile and cheese. It comes with a choice of country spuds, toast, or pancakes.

Among the standard choices are French toast, a short stack (3 pancakes), and a stack (5 pancakes). There is also the chicken fried steak and egg selection. Biscuits and gravy with a side of two pieces of bacon or sausage will be sure to fill you up.

For the young or young at heart, Happy's features Mickey Mouse pancakes. Who wouldn't like to have a plate full of a delectable Disney character? The kids are delighted by the fun shape and the parents are thrilled the kids are actually eating their breakfast! For the family with children, Happy's is the perfect spot to dine.

Next time you are on your way to the Caverns or just want to have a great breakfast while in Carlsbad, be sure to follow the smiley faces to Happy's.

Recommended Reading: Boys will be boys, but when mama expresses herself with a heavy hand and a loving heart, they tend to behave. In the true historical account, *Ma'am Jones of the Pecos* by Eve Ball, we follow the life of Barbara Jones, a real pioneer woman who managed to raise nine sons and one daughter in Seven Rivers, New Mexico, now a ghost town located between Carlsbad and Artesia. Seven Rivers was once large enough to give Eddy (Carlsbad) a run for its money in their bid for county seat and in its time was known as one of the most violent towns in the west. Local lore claims no one died of natural causes in Seven Rivers. In the midst of the chaos surrounding her, Ma'am Jones ran a trading post, befriended Billy the Kid, suffered the tragic loss of several of her sons to the hands of the violence and was one of the few people with "doctorin'" skills around, all the while making the best pies in the region.

After Breakfast: Visit the Living Desert Zoo & Gardens State Park, an indoor/outdoor living museum displaying more than 40 native animal species and hundreds of succulent plants from around the world. www.emnrd.state.nm.us/PRD/LivingDesert.htm

Jack's

19 Carlsbad Caverns Hwy.
White's City, NM 88268
(800) 228-3767
(575) 785-2291
www.whitescity.com

Kid Component:**
Prices: $$

L ocated at the mouth of the Carlsbad Cavern National Park, White's City has provided eager travelers with entertainment including curio shops, museums, a water park, and restaurants since 1931. One of these restaurants frequented by tourists is Jack's, named appropriately after Jack White, Jr., one of the founders of White's City.

Jack's is a diner-style setting featuring huge photographs by renowned Cavern photographer Ennis Creed "Tex" Helm. Helm, originally a newspaper photographer, was sponsored by Sylvania to demonstrate the worth of their flashbulbs. We were told by the enthusiastic owners, Charles White and Mary Duggar, that he used 2,400 flashbulbs connected by nearly three miles of cable to expose a single picture in the Big Room of the Carlsbad Caverns. We were also shown an article in the National Geographic that stated the exposure was the most vivid flash since the atomic bomb was detonated in 1945.

You do not have to worry about blinding flashes at Jack's. Place your order at the counter before entering the dining room and get your soft drinks at the fountain area around the corner. A window seat will give you breathtaking views of the Guadalupe Mountains and the native plants surrounding White's City. If you get there early enough, we are told the resident deer may greet you.

Jack's cook, Sammy Martinez, is known for his cinnamon rolls and *huevos rancheros*. Martinez enjoys throwing in a special or two during the week just to shake things up, so keep an eye out for these extra special specials. The tried and true favorites include a two egg plate served with bacon, ham, or sausage, hash browns, and toast and jelly. As with most New Mexico restaurants, a breakfast burrito is always available. Unique items on the menu are the six half-dollar pancakes with bacon, ham, or sausage—a favorite with the kids. Biscuits and gravy with hash browns are also offered. Maybe your taste buds will call you towards the three egg omelet or the scrumptious French toast. Lighter fare includes hot or cold cereal, English muffins, or bagels. No matter what you order, you won't be disappointed.

As advertised, Jack's will expedite your meal so you can have a full day to enjoy the wondrous Carlsbad Caverns. The hearty breakfast will sustain you to the top of the Cavern's "Appetite Hill" and beyond.

Recommended Reading: What better way to enjoy a relaxing meal in White's City than to do it while reading *Carlsbad Caverns National Park New Mexico: Its Early Explorations* as told by Jim White. This book can be purchased at the Curio Shop and will give you insight into the early Carlsbad Cavern exploration as only Jim White could tell. Fascinating!

After Breakfast: White's City is a great destination for families looking for some fun at the gateway of one of the world's most stunning wonders. Don't forget while you are there to indulge in Mrs. White's delectable fudge sold at the Curio Shop.

Pecos River Café

409 S. Canal
Carlsbad, NM 88220
(575) 887-8882

Breakfast Hours:
Monday-Friday 6:30am-3pm
Kid Component:***
Prices: $

Old-world charm and home-cooked meals await you in the Pecos River Café. Owner Diana Czerny continues a family tradition of delicious food prepared and presented with care. She is on-site every day overseeing and working alongside her staff to provide a pleasant dining experience for everyone who visits. You will see the cooks behind the counter preparing everything fresh on the spot; your food won't be something scooped out of a warming pan or re-heated in the microwave.

The Pecos River Café has a well-deserved reputation for great tasting food and good service. A wide variety of typical American breakfast fare is offered as well as some Mexican-American breakfast entrées. Specialties of the house include enormous, fluffy cinnamon rolls baked fresh daily, *huevos rancheros*, egg burritos, and country ham and eggs (a thick slice of ham, two eggs cooked any style; and your choice of pancakes, fresh biscuits and gravy, or toast).

Red and green chile sauces are made in the kitchen every day and add a fresh and spicy bite to your entrée. *Huevos rancheros* comes with two eggs smothered in cheese and the chile sauce of your choice. Beans and hash browns are included. The hearty breakfast burrito contains two scrambled eggs and chile, all rolled in a flour tortilla and garnished with cheddar cheese, lettuce, and tomato, along with two sausage links, hash browns, and pinto beans.

A three-egg omelet is guaranteed to fill you up. A basic egg and cheese omelet comes with toast and hash-brown potatoes. You can substitute an English muffin or bagel for the toast. A ham, bacon, or sausage omelet is priced right, as is the western omelet with chopped ham, green pepper, and onion.

On the sweeter side try the pancakes or the Texas-size crispy French toast, both served with maple syrup and butter.

The Pecos River Café is a very popular breakfast spot with local diners, and menu items are available for carry out.

Recommended Reading: If an exciting thriller works up your appetite, read Nevada Barr's *Blind Descent*, one of a series of novels set in national parks. Barr's protagonist, Anna Pigeon, ends up in Lechuguila Cave, part of the Carlsbad Caverns cave system. The dramatic rescue of a stranded spelunker kicks off the action, and soon Ms. Pigeon is involved in the investigation of two murders.

After Breakfast: Plan ahead to explore Lechuguila Cave at Carlsbad, or take a self-guided walking tour of the Caverns. Carlsbad Caverns has awe-inspiring caves for people of every age, interest, and ability. www.nps.gov/cave

Roja's Mexican Grill and Restaurant

2704 San Jose Blvd.
Carlsbad, NM 88220
(575) 885-2146
(575) 885-5478

Breakfast Hours:
Tuesday-Sunday 8am-8pm
Kid Component:***
Prices: $$

A tiny bit off the beaten path, Roja's Mexican Grill and Restaurant is well worth the extra effort you may spend in finding it. Ask any local for directions, or if you're the adventurous type, just take the small "Y" on South Canal Street across from Danny's Place and Furr's Cafeteria, which quickly exits Canal at that point. You will be below and beside a bridge on San Jose Blvd. that you will follow for approximately two miles passing the Fiesta Drive-In Theater (the last of a dying breed of operating outdoor movie theaters). Cross a small irrigation ditch, top a hill, and Roja's will be on your left hand side. Even if the gravel parking lot looks full, try it anyway. Owner Tomas Rojas expanded the restaurant from its original one room status to gladly accommodate the overflow.

Viva Mexico! You'll swear you've just stepped across the border into Mexico as you enter Roja's. Your nose will tell you right off the bat what your stomach is in for: heaven on a plate. A lively southwest-themed décor accented with the colors of the Mexican flag greets you as you step through the front doors (guarded by Pancho Villa). As their sign states, you're in for the "Taste of Mexico."

If you enjoy people watching, Roja's attracts customers from all walks of life. You never know who will drop by. We were told that if you frequent this restaurant enough, the waitress will know your order without asking.

For the diner who's hungry for a hearty, spicy breakfast, Roja's offers a delicious full breakfast menu, complemented by fresh homemade salsa with chips, refried beans, a tortilla and potatoes. Many Mexican favorites are represented, such as a large assortment of breakfast burritos, steak and eggs, *huevos con chorizo*, *huevos rancheros*, a red *enchilada montado* chicken or beef smothered in red sauce and covered with two fried eggs), *machaca* (dried shredded beef with two scrambled eggs), *huevos con carne* (red or green chunk beef tip with chile con carne served with two eggs), and a Mexican omelet topped with tomatoes, onions, jalapeños, and cheese. But don't feel left out if your palate prefers a more subdued breakfast, Roja's also offers standard American breakfast fare as well.

Give yourself some time to savor the tastes and atmosphere. Roja's is a family owned and operated establishment, with family being the key word. We found Roja's to have a very child-friendly vibe. You'll feel like one of the group as Roja's exemplifies the hometown eatery. If you are eating alone, try to snag a table close to the front plate glass windows because they sport a fabulous view of the Guadalupe Mountains, with El Capitan in the distance.

Recommended Reading: Red or green? New Mexico's official question is magnificently illustrated in the *Chile Chronicles: Tales of a New Mexico Harvest* by Carmella Padilla featuring the spectacular photography of Jack Parsons. As New Mexicans, we take chile for granted as a staple for our diet. This book follows the entire chile production process from field to table.

After Breakfast: Head to the Carlsbad Museum at 418 W. Fox Street where you'll find exhibits of Mogollon Anasazi ceramics and works by Gustave Baumann, Glenna Goodacre, Peter Hurd and Roderick Mead. During your visit, drop into the Carlsbad Public Library located right next to the museum. The library has occupied this location for more than 100 years!

Chama

Elk Horn Café

2289 S State Road 17
Chama, NM 87520
(575) 756-2229

Breakfast Hours:
Daily 7am-noon
Kid Component:***
Price: $$

Given the name of this restaurant, you might expect to see lots of elk horns inside, and you won't be disappointed. But there are also great train photographs covering a good portion of the wood paneling. Bird feeders mounted outside the building next to the windows let you spy on a variety of feathered friends. If the season and/or weather are right, dine out on the deck, where you can hear the sounds of the nearby Chama River and even closer *acequia* (irrigation canal).

Featuring a great big "Good Morning" right at the top, the menu is formatted with headings such as Breakfast is Served, Eggs Plus, Three Egg Omelets, Hot off the Griddle, and Drinks & Sides. Offerings include cereal, oatmeal (plain or with blueberries or brown sugar and raisins), yogurt, hand-held burrito, biscuits and gravy, and the Giant Cinnamon Roll. Under Eggs Plus, The American with two eggs any style, potatoes, toast, or English muffin, comes in three versions depending on your meat wishes. Also in this category you'll find pork chop/*chorizo*/steak and eggs; grilled corned beef hash; *huevos rancheros*, *carne adovada*, and a smothered breakfast burrito. Three kinds of three-egg omelets are available including the Elk Horn Omelet that features ham, sautéed mushrooms, avocado and Swiss cheese.

Items Hot off the Griddle include buttermilk pancakes, French toast, and chocolate chip pancakes topped with peanut butter.

While awaiting the arrival of your entrée and assuming you're accompanied by congenial company, order a Giant Cinnamon Roll. Living up to its name by nearly covering the plate, the Giant Cinnamon Roll's characteristic spiral is barely visible under a thick coat of frosting. Plan to share or take part home: never attempt to eat the whole thing by yourself at one sitting. These colossal confections go fast, hence the menu admonition "when available" in fine print.

Recommended Reading: Kids can go along for the ride with the mascot of the Cumbres & Toltec Railroad in *Cinder Bear and the Christmas Train* by part-time Chama resident Jill Lane.

After Breakfast: The Cumbres & Toltec Railroad transports riders across state lines (and historic lines too!) from late spring through fall with an occasional holiday trip in the snow.
www.cumbrestoltec.com

High Country Restaurant

2663 S Highway 84-64
Chama, NM 87520
(575) 756-2229

Breakfast Hours:
Daily 7am-noon
Kid Component:***
Price: $$

If you're lucky enough to find yourself in Chama on a Sunday morning, don't bother asking the tall, stocky fellow wearing a white shirt, black vest, string tie, cowboy hat, and boots stationed by the door to the High Country Restaurant for a recommendation about a good place to have breakfast. Definitely the strong, silent type, and bearing more than a passing resemblance to an iconic movie hero, he never says a word. Not a clue escapes his lips. Perhaps this is because he's carved out of a log, the bottom of which he's still standing on. If he could talk, though, he'd no doubt tell you you've come to the right spot.

As you step into the banquet-hall style dining room, you'll realize immediately you're onto something. No sooner are you seated than your server appears to take your beverage order and invite you to proceed to the breakfast buffet. The omelet station is a floor show in itself. Presiding over an array of four burners and two waffle irons, the cook displays the skill and timing of a juggler. Concoctions including chopped bell peppers, green chile, jalapeños, cheese, mushrooms, ham, tomato, and/or sausage are folded over perfectly at the precise moment of doneness and slide smoothly from pan to plate. Waffle batter is transformed in minutes into crispy golden brown cakes.

Meanwhile, in another part of the room, pancakes, sausage (patties and links), bacon, gravy, beans, sausage gravy, biscuits, hash browns, salsa, and chile sauce (red and green) are kept piping hot. Yet another table features bread, English muffins, and bagels for toasting (toaster provided), syrup, jam, and butter.

The chef makes a delicious compote from blueberries, strawberries, and liqueur. Served warm, it's a superb topper for waffles, pancakes, or the made-from-scratch biscuits. Whipped cream is provided as a further enhancement.

Swinging barroom-style doors lead to the kitchen and they swish practically non-stop as the wait staff keeps the omelet wizard supplied with ingredients, replenishes the buffet, provides refills on coffee, and in general pays close attention to the needs of the guests.

The extremely reasonable all-in-one price for the brunch includes beverages. Children eat for less than half the adult rate.

Maybe, as you walk out exclaiming about your fabulous meal, you just might recall who the carved cowboy by the door reminds you of. Perhaps the tune "Do not forsake me, oh my darling" floats on the breeze. Be happy you got here in time. Brunch ends at high noon.

Recommended Reading: Speaking of western movies, New Mexico author Max Evans' classic 1961 novel *The Hi–Lo Country* was made into a movie in 1998.

After Breakfast: There are lots of reasons to visit Chama: at least two annual Fairs (Author and Quilt), superb hunting and fishing.

Rebecca's at The Lodge

Corona Place
Cloudcroft, NM 88317
(575) 682-3131
www.thelodgeresort.com/
dining.cfm

Breakfast hours: Monday-
Saturday 7am-10:30am,
Sunday 7am-10am
Kid component:***
Price: $$$

Ghostly laughing, spontaneously lit fireplace fires, mysteriously moving ashtrays, late night phone calls (and when you answer no one is there); these are all tricks the resident ghost at The Lodge at Cloudcroft has been known to play on unsuspecting guests. The dining room that serves breakfast every day at The Lodge is named in honor of the ghostly spirit believed to haunt the halls; Rebecca.

Rebecca's story is a tale of jealousy, beauty, and tragedy. As the legend of Rebecca is told, she was a beautiful chambermaid who was murdered by her jealous lumberjack boyfriend after he caught her in the arms of another man. Those who have seen Rebecca describe her as flirtatious and mischievous, and many believe she is in search of a new lover. A stained glass window of Rebecca with her flowing red hair can be seen in the breakfast room at Rebecca's.

The ghost of Rebecca may entertain you at unpredictable times during your visit to The Lodge, but the sights that are predictable and can be seen with the human eye are the highlight of dining at Rebecca's restaurant. Waking up early to eat breakfast at this romantic restaurant is easy. The breakfast seating area is lined with giant west-facing windows, providing one of the best views available from any restaurant in New Mexico. The hotel and dining room sit atop the Sacramento Mountains and overlook the Tularosa Basin. While sitting in your comfortable chair at the breakfast table, you will enjoy the beautiful gardens and koi pond cared for by The Lodge. On clear sky mornings you can look through the pine trees and across the valley. To the south you will spot White Sands strung along the valley floor.

The views are truly awe-inspiring, but when the breakfast arrives, your attention will quickly be drawn back to the dining table. Wait staff dressed in black and white uniforms bring pitchers full of steaming hot coffee and glasses filled with bright orange juice.

One of our favorite dishes at Rebecca's is the crab cakes with poached eggs. The crab cakes are a deliciously decadent breakfast treat. The eggs are always perfectly done and served with potatoes and fresh fruit. We also highly recommend the Lumberjack, a large entrée that includes biscuits topped with creamy gravy, fried eggs, and sausage. Another special item on the menu is the trout with eggs. The trout is served fresh from the stream and comes with potatoes and biscuits.

Enjoying a relaxing breakfast at Rebecca's is the perfect start to any day. The flawless breakfast entrées served in this high altitude paradise should not be missed.

Recommended Reading: Are you intrigued by Rebecca's spirit? Scare up a copy of *New Mexico Ghost Stories* by Antonio R. Garcez.

After Breakfast: Take a short 2.5 mile hike on the Trestle Trail. The trail begins at a replica of Cloudcroft's depot, and winds down to the Mexican Canyon Trestle. The wooden train trestle was a vital part of the Cloud-Climbing Railroad that once ran up and down the Sacramento Mountains.
www.traillink.com/ViewTrail.aspx?AcctID=6016589

Española

Ançelina's Restaurant

1226 North Railroad Avenue
Española, NM 87532
(505) 753-8543

Breakfast Hours: Daily 7am-11am
Kid Component:***
Prices: $$

As a way of coping with their son's death from leukemia, the Gutierrez family opened Angelina's Restaurant in 1984. The Gutierrez's son's love of his mother's red chile and ground beef and beans encouraged her to open a restaurant. In the beginning, Angelina retained a full-time job with the Española Public Schools, taking her lunch breaks at the restaurant where she cooked and served meals with her husband and daughter.

The popularity of Angelina's prompted the construction of a custom space into which she moved in 1998. The new space with its white walls and wood trim has an open and airy feel. The décor has roosters of many types, live plants, and art for sale.

The specialties include locally grown lamb, beef, and produce for a uniquely native northern New Mexican flavor experience. Among the breakfast offerings are *huevos rancheros*, red chile pork, *puelitas* (a hot skillet with hash browns, grilled vegetables, cheese, red or green chile, and ham, *chorizo* or grilled lamb), and Angelina's own delicious creation: a breakfast *enchilada* (an ample corn tortilla with cheese, beans, ground beef, rolled and smothered in cheese with your choice of chile).

Now retired from the school system, Angelina is trying to retire from the restaurant and allow her grandchildren to run the family business. They refuse to let her retire, so she keeps dreaming.

All of Angelina's offerings are prepared on site daily. The fresh, hand-made delights from Angelina's kitchen will keep you coming back.

Recommended Reading: *Tomás and the Library Lady* by Pat Mora, acclaimed children's author and part-time New Mexico resident, reflects the same pride in bilingual heritage that Angelina's Restaurant conveys with food.

After Breakfast: You can make a splash at the Española Library. There's an indoor swimming pool sharing the building with the public library. www.youseemore.com/espanola

Jo Ann's Ranch O Casados Restaurant

938 North Riverside Drive
(Highway 68)
Española, NM 87532
(505) 753-1334
www.joannsranchocasados.com

Breakfast Hours:
Monday-Thursday 6am-8pm,
Friday-Saturday 6am-9pm,
Sunday 7am-3pm
Kid Component:***
Prices: $$

Internationally known Casados Farms is the supplier for all the locally-grown ingredients for Jo Ann's world-class foods. Jo Ann personally hand roasts and peels all the green chile used in her recipes. Family owned and operated since 1984, Jo Ann's slogan of "[Heart Shape] At First Bite" adorns her bumper stickers seen all over the world. Customers have told her of seeing the bumper stickers on a backpack in Nepal, a cab in Rome, and a van in Australia.

In the early 1980s, Española suffered a dearth of traditional Northern New Mexican cuisine restaurants. Jo Ann stepped up to fill the void providing excellent food at affordable prices. She moved into a building that once housed a Sears catalog shop and began serving the foods her family had been supplying to restaurants from Texas through New Mexico, Wyoming, and across Colorado.

Using the four-hundred year-old recipes of the Casados family, Jo Ann strives to make everything old new again. She added vegetarian selections to her menu to serve Española's growing Sikh community.

Soon after its opening, Jo Ann's became the place to eat in Española. She eventually expanded the small space of her original restaurant adding a banquet room and more seating. The local Toastmasters had a surge in membership when they reserved seating for their early Saturday morning meetings in Jo Ann's dining room.

After a short sabbatical, Jo Ann opened the restaurant in its current location in 2003. Her loyal customers returned and brought with them many friends.

Local artists display and sell their works at Jo Ann's. Fine examples of carving, painting and tin smithing abound on the walls and windowsills. The art is complemented by the hand-finished pine tables and Spanish carved reception desk.

The entire menu is served all day. One can get a full or half order of many of the house specialties. Most popular breakfast items include *huevos rancheros*, breakfast burritos, and *carne adovada*. Jo Ann's *carne adovada* is so good, it has been flown to New York on demand for an anniversary dinner.

Over the past 25 years, Jo Ann's has become a part of many families' stories. A trip through New Mexico must include a visit to Jo Ann's for tourists and natives alike. The hand-made *tamales*, *sopapillas*, and tortillas have the taste of sitting in your *abuela's* (gramma's) kitchen. Ms. Casados calls her customers "the prize that makes your business."

Recommended Reading: *El Santo Queso: The Holy Cheese* is a collection of stories by the late Española author and poet, Jim Sagel. His uniquely New Mexican humor is present in his bilingual writings that match the strange political realities of Rio Arriba County. Jim Sagel was a frequent patron of Jo Ann's.

After Breakfast: Take some time to visit the Misión y Convento, a church that was reconstructed based on excavations done on the site in the 1940s. The original church was built by the Spanish in the 1590s as part of the settlement of San Gabriel.
www.plazadeespanola.com/mision.php

Lovin' Oven Bakery Shoppe

107 North Riverside Drive
(Highway 68)
Española, NM 87532
(505) 753-5461

Breakfast Hours:
Monday-Saturday 6am-noon
Kid Component:**
Prices: $

Though not technically a restaurant, the Lovin' Oven serves up excellent pastries, doughnuts, and gourmet coffee for those on-the-go. Limited seating is available inside, and drive-thru service is an option for procuring Lovin' Oven's hand-made delights.

The baker and owner, Dino Martinez, is nicknamed "Saint Dino of the Doughnuts" for all his generous philanthropic work in Española. Whether it is donating fresh doughnuts to the semi-annual Española clean-up days, a full sheet cake for the Española Public Library's 30th anniversary, or some of his world-famous *bizcochitos* for the children's summer reading program, his cheerful outlook and merry demeanor are graciously shared along with the goodies.

After baking to rave reviews from his family and friends, Martinez was reluctantly persuaded to open his own bakery. Having spent years in the restaurant business, he found that he truly loved making wonderful things to eat and has been at the same location since February 1991.

Dino's *bizcochitos* are some of the finest cookies we have ever tasted, a sentiment shared by people across the Española Valley. Each Christmas, the community streams into his bakery, picking up their standing orders of holiday *bizcochitos* and placing orders for the following year.

Right behind the *bizcochitos*, running a very close second in popularity, are the Lovin' Oven's *pastelitos*. *Pastelitos* are a traditional Spanish hand-held fruit pastry, less sweet than their fruit pie cousin.

Seasonal fruits blend perfectly with the flakey crust for a lighter, portable alternative to a slice of pie.

When he's not baking, St. Dino is at the library or between the pages of a cookbook researching recipes to ever improve his already scrumptious offerings.

The Lovin' Oven makes all of their breads, cookies, doughnuts, cakes, and *pastelitos* from scratch. Absolutely no mixes or prepared ingredients are used. This care and attention to detail comes through loud and clear in the taste. This self-taught master of the craft beautifully decorates his cakes for weddings, graduations, birthdays, and special events.

Come taste the love and tradition baked in to every bite.

Recommended Reading: *The Española Valley Cookbook: Recipes from Three Cultures: Spanish, Anglo, Indian*, now in its 4th updated printing, was compiled by the Española Hospital Auxiliary. Dino Martinez contributed to the latest edition.

After Breakfast: Visit the Bond House at the historic Plaza de Española. This historic home was built by the Frank Bond family, a family that came to New Mexico from Canada and opened a mercantile in the late 1800s. www.plazadeespanola.com/bond.php

Aurelia's Diner

2502 E. Historic Highway 66
Gallup, NM
(505) 726-2800

Breakfast Hours: Daily 7am-
11am and 2pm-7pm
Kid Component:***
Prices: $

Tom and Michelle Duckett opened Aurelia's Diner in 2006. Tom, a true entrepreneur, had always dreamed of owning a restaurant. The diner is named after Tom's grandmother, Aurelia, who helped inspire Tom's love of cooking.

All the recipes are family recipes. In fact, the diner is a family affair. Tom's mother Rosalie gets up at 4:00 every morning to "do the chile." Her *chile guerrito* (blonde chile) is sold as Rosalie's Special and has been described as "the most delicious thing you've ever put in your mouth." Other breakfast entrées include smothered breakfast burritos with your choice of fillings including *chorizo, huevos rancheros*, and omelets any way you want them. The favorite entrée for many diners is Aurelia's Morning Special (two eggs with hash browns, a choice of bacon, sausage, ham, or *chorizo*, toast, a choice of red or green chile) served with a cup of coffee.

Aurelia's is located directly on Historic Route 66 and has a great view of the hogbacks that run along Route 66 in the area. The morning sun makes the view especially spectacular, casting shadows on the distinctive rock formations.

The restaurant has a sparkling clean 60s diner look with red and white décor. The health inspector has been overheard to say it is the cleanest establishment in western New Mexico. Tom's love of memorabilia has provided much of the ambience for the diner. Some of his favorites include antique Coke and Pepsi machines, a Marilyn Monroe contract from one of her early movies, and a hot wheels car in its original package. He also has some genuine Elvis Presley concert ticket stubs.

Celebrity Anecdote: Country singer George Strait was stranded in Gallup during one of the many times I-40 was shut down. The highway patrol routed his tour bus from Grants down through Ramah and back up to I-40 in Gallup. The bus driver said he was sure they were never going to see civilization again. When the entourage finally reached Gallup, they were starving. Tom closed the restaurant to everyone but them so they could have a hot meal and a place where they could have some peace and quiet. Strait, who had a stuffed *sopapilla*, said they have the best chile on Route 66.

Even though Aurelia's location dictates that a large number of tourists are included in their customer base, a sizable number of local folks frequent the diner.

Recommend Reading: A primary resource for students studying New Mexico History is *Gallup, New Mexico, U.S.A.: Our Story* by Sally Noe. Noe published this book in 1997 after many years teaching New Mexico history at Gallup High School. In addition, Sally spends many happy hours dining at Aurelia's Diner with friends and family.

After Breakfast: Take some time to walk around downtown Gallup and enjoy the many murals the city has commissioned in recent years through the Downtown Mural Project. Visit the Chamber of Commerce and pick up a walking tour map of the murals.
gallupnm.org/residents/murals.cfm

Earl's Restaurant

1400 E. US 66
Gallup, NM 87301
(505) 853-4201

Breakfast Hours:
Daily 6am-11am
Kid Component:***
Prices: $$

Earl's had a small start. It began in 1947 as a restaurant with seating for seven. Since its early days, Earl's has been a local hangout. In 1979 Sharon Richards (a waitress at Earl's since 1968) put her car up for collateral to purchase the restaurant from the original owner, Earl Nelson.

After the Richards family purchased the restaurant, its popularity continued to grow which allowed the restaurant to expand and open in its new building in 1990. Since then, Earl's has continued to serve homemade food and New Mexican fare to locals and tourists alike to the tune of 10,000 cups of coffee and 800 pounds of green chile a week.

Besides the bustle of the restaurant, Earl's is also home to dozens of Native American artisans who set up each day in the breezeway built around the restaurant especially for selling goods. If you are too hungry and pass by the breezeway sheltering the tables of jewelry, pottery, and beadwork without buying something, you have not missed your chance to shop. The artisans circulate unobtrusively through the restaurant stopping at each table offering diners the unique opportunity to eat and shop at the same time.

Hearty breakfast fare includes pancakes, French toast, and typical hash browns. New Mexican favorites include breakfast burritos, *enchiladas* and eggs, sausage *enchiladas* and *huevos rancheros*. The coffee here is great and the wait staff will not allow you to drain your cup no matter how long you sit and visit with friends and family. After 11:00 am you can get limited breakfast offerings including steak and eggs, pancakes, and more of those tasty *huevos rancheros*.

Recommended Reading: *The Seed Trilogy* written by Philip Stevenson (a blacklisted screenwriter during the McCarthy era) under the pseudonym Lars Lawrence is a set of novels based on a true incident of civil unrest in Gallup during the 1930's. The story begins when a local politician buys up land where impoverished miners live and attempts to collect exorbitant rent. The Mexican-American miners protest and after being arrested and jailed, a riot takes place and both law enforcement and miners are killed. Left-wing organizers arrive in the fictional town of Reata and lots of intrigue follows.

After Breakfast: You might want to continue shopping at the Gallup trading posts. We recommend stops at Richardson's Trading Company and Tobe Turpin's Trading Post.
www.richardsontrading.com/, www.tobeturpens.com

El Rancho Hotel and Restaurant

1000 E. US 66
Gallup, NM 87301
(800) 543-6351
www.elranchohotel.com

Breakfast Hours: Monday-
Saturday 6:30am-11:30am,
Sunday 6:30am-1pm
Kid Component:**
Prices: $$

The El Rancho Hotel was built in 1937 by D.W. Griffith, a man with Hollywood connections. The hotel became home to movie stars in the 1940s through the 1960s as they made western movies in the Gallup area. Movie star guests include Ronald Reagan, Spencer Tracy, Katharine Hepburn, and Kirk Douglas.

Hundreds of autographed photos of Hollywood stars line the walls of the El Rancho lobby. The hotel décor includes cliché old western furnishings, Navajo rugs, and trophy animal heads, all adding to the historic mystique of this once glorious hotel.

One of the breakfast house specials (called Regional Delights on the El Rancho menu) is *atole*, a blue corn hot cereal. *Huevos rancheros* are another local favorite. If you want your *huevos rancheros* cooked up in a special way, ask the staff—they are always willing to accommodate special orders. For example, many folks choose to have the *huevos rancheros* served with potatoes rather than the traditional rice and beans. The El Rancho's potatoes are famous; rather than hash browns, they serve potatoes fried in large pieces.

Steak and eggs, along with Spanish and western omelets are other breakfast offerings that are favorites of those who eat here often.

A meal at the El Rancho is near the top of our list of "funky" dining experiences. The aging hotel and restaurant have the distinct feel of glorious western ranch luxury from a time-gone-by.

Recommend Reading: Laurance Linford leads Tony Hillerman aficionados to the Four Corners locations described in Hillerman's novels in his book *Tony Hillerman's Navajoland: Hideouts, Haunts, and Havens in the Joe Leaphorn and Jim Chee Mysteries.*

After Breakfast: Using the book above, look for the truth in fiction by visiting some of the locations Hillerman mentioned in his stories.

Jemez Springs

Ridgeback Café

38710 Highway 126
Jemez Springs, NM 87025
(575) 829-3322

Breakfast Hours: Tuesday–
Sunday, 7:30am-11am
Kid Component:***
Price: $$

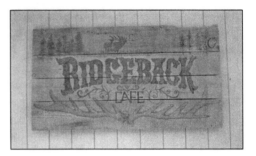

Maybe you've come up to the mystical Jemez Mountains to see Jemez Pueblo. Perhaps the rock-climbing and fishing opportunities have beckoned. Is it the history at Jemez State Monument, or the healing waters of Jemez Springs that draw you to this elevation? Could it be the lovely picnic sites at Battleship Rock, or concerts at Hummingbird Music Camp? How about the fabulous Valles Caldera National Preserve, with its iconic Valle Grande expansively spread out along State Road 4, hinting at hidden treasures just beyond the tree-covered peaks or above the timberline?

The Ridgeback Café in La Cueva at the junction of State Roads 4 and 126 is the perfect spot for a hearty breakfast before heading out to explore the wonders of the Jemez Mountains.

Rustic is the perfect term to describe this cozy place. A huge elevated wood-burning stove dominates the dining room. It exudes coziness, not to mention welcome warmth during the winter months. The predominant decorative motif is antlers (this is elk country, after all). There are some pretty spectacular racks, and details are provided as to who procured them and when. If you manage to clean your plate you'll even see elk portrayed on the dishes. The secondary decorative motif is photos of wildlife, accent on the *wild*. There's a particularly unnerving photo of a bobcat that seems to be watching every bite you take. If you're in his line of sight, you might want to change seats. There are some pictures of bears, too.

Speaking of bears, the menu offers a trio of entrées that seem perfect for that famous ursine family who encountered Miss Goldilocks, the poster child of picky eaters. Baby Bear might enjoy the "Itty-Bitty" (one savory egg cooked to your liking, one slice of crispy bacon or one plump sausage patty, toast or one homemade biscuit). The French toast (thick slices of Texas toast dipped in vanilla and cinnamon with a sprinklin' of powdered sugar) sounds like something Mama Bear would love. Papa Bear isn't left out with the "Big Papa" (it is a mega-version of the "Itty-Bitty" with the addition of hash browns). As for Goldilocks herself, I'd bet that after she gobbled down the Breakfast Sandwich— two eggs cooked your way with bacon, chopped green chile, and melted cheese on your choice of toasted bread, she'd probably exclaim "That was just right!"

Barely resistible are the Ridgeback's other offerings, including rib eye and eggs, ham and eggs, and chicken fried steak and eggs. Additionally, there is a nice selection of omelets and the "Little Stuff": pancakes, jumbo cinnamon roll, and biscuits and gravy.

Recommended Reading: When a little cow ignores his mother's advice and climbs to the top of a mountain, he finds himself tired, hungry, cold, and in need of a fast way to get back to his mother in their beautiful meadow in the bi-lingual children's book *The Little Cow in Valle Grande/El Becerrito en Valle Grande* by Skillman "Kim" Hunter with evocative illustrations by Mary Sundstrom. Adults will get a taste of the spiritual and mystical facets of the Jemez Mountains in Rudolfo Anaya's *Jemez Spring*, the last of four mystery novels featuring private detective Sonny Baca. The book opens in the bathhouse at Jemez Springs, which is a stone's throw from the Jemez Springs Public Library.

After Breakfast: Head to the Valles Caldera for hiking trails and photographing some of the most amazing sites nature has to offer. Visit the website to plan your trip.
www.vallescaldera.gov

Las Cruces

Andele Restaurante

2184 S. Highway 28 (Avenida de Mesilla)
Mesilla, NM 88046
(575) 526-9631
www.andelerestaurante.com

Breakfast Hours:
Daily 8am-11am
Kid Component:***
Prices: $

Y ou will enjoy getting yourself out of bed for breakfast at Andele's, a small café just blocks away from the historic Mesilla Plaza.

While dining in this locally owned restaurant, you can watch cooks in the kitchen prepare meals. If you are too busy to stop for a sit-down-breakfast, Andele's offers breakfast for folks on-the-run at the walk-up take-out window.

The *huevos rancheros* are a local favorite, and especially good (two any style eggs on two warm corn tortillas smothered with *ranchera* sauce and topped with shredded cheese). The *huevos rancheros* are served with refried beans, home fried potatoes, and a warm flour tortilla. Other breakfast delights range from biscuits and gravy to *menudo* (available Saturday and Sunday only).

Recommended Reading: New Mexico has cast its spell on people for hundreds of years. In 1976 Tony Hillerman compiled essays by Ernie Pyle, Oliver La Farge, D.H. Lawrence, and others who have felt the power of New Mexico landscapes and cultures. These treasured writings can be read in *The Spell of New Mexico* edited by Tony Hillerman.

After Breakfast: Old Mesilla is a required stop for most visitors in the Las Cruces area. This old village has a long and rich history dating back to the sixteenth history. Today Old Mesilla features shops, historic buildings, restaurants, a movie theater, and museums.
www.oldmesilla.org

Dick's Café

2305 S. Valley Dr.
Las Cruces, NM 88005
(575) 524-1360
www.dickscafe.net

Breakfast Hours:
Daily 7am-11am
Kid Component:***
Prices: $

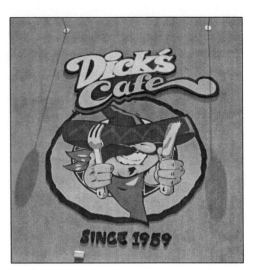

For over 50 years Dick's has been in business serving food that southern New Mexicans love. Dick's was originally founded by Ace Perez's grandfather at a truck stop; it moved to the south Valley Drive location and developed into a full fledged restaurant when Interstate 10 was built.

At Dick's you will find a cross section of all people living in southern New Mexico. It's a favorite restaurant for the biker crowd, farmers and ranchers in town for shopping, students and professors from New Mexico State University, newly relocated retirees, tourists visiting White Sands, NASA employees, and anyone else who likes just plain good food and an easy-going atmosphere.

At a recent breakfast we found the hotcakes light, eggs done as ordered, and hash browns crispy but not greasy. Service was friendly, and the restaurant filled up quickly with fellow diners as we ate.

If you are hungry you will find a wide selection of burritos, omelets with nine possible fillings, and *chorizo* and eggs. Egg substitute is available for the heart-conscious.

Recommended Reading: *A Place Like No Other: People of an Enchanted Land* by Daryl A. Black reminds us that you can meet anyone at Dick's. It is a wonderful photographic composite of the kind of people who inhabit our state from north to south and east to west.

After Breakfast: One of Las Cruces' newest attractions is the New Mexico Farm and Ranch Heritage Museum, a state institution exhibiting agricultural life and its history in New Mexico from earliest times to the present. Exhibits feature equipment, well-described agricultural practices, and live animals.
www.nmfarmandranchmuseum.org

Enrique's Mexican Food

830 W. Picacho Ave.
Las Cruces, NM 88005
(575) 647-0240

Breakfast Hours:
Monday-Saturday 7am-noon,
Sunday 7:30am-noon
Kid Component:*
Prices: $

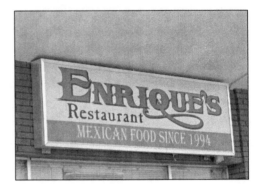

Enrique has been serving his style of reasonably priced, great tasting Mexican food in the same location since 1994. This is definitely a working class neighborhood kind of place with little in the way of atmosphere, but the food is great. Enrique himself usually takes your order and a more cheerful easy-going fellow would be hard to imagine.

There are eight items on the breakfast menu. They range from the *huevos rancheros* to the steak and eggs. All entrées come with chips and salsa, an excellent beginning to the day.

On our most recent visit we had the *huevos rancheros*. They came with refried beans, lettuce, and a dollop of guacamole plus two hot flour tortillas on the side. You can custom order your *huevos rancheros* by asking for cheese, corn tortillas instead of flour tortillas, and the eggs can be served on top of your tortilla—just ask. Enrique told us the red salsa on the eggs was the hottest they had available. It had a great taste with a bit of a smoky flavor, but hot it was not.

The *machaca* is excellent also. *Machaca,* called *chilaquiles* by some, is a dish with scrambled eggs, chopped onions, green peppers, *chorizo*, and tortilla chips.

Enrique's is definitely unpretentious. You will be most comfortable arriving at this diner in jeans and a t-shirt. This is also a place to practice your Español. Enrique and the two or three other staff speak English, as do most of the customers, but Spanish is what you hear when you open the door.

Recommended Reading: Laura Esquivel's *Like Water for Chocolate* is a passionately told tale of magic, forbidden love, parental tyranny, and Mexican history. An undercurrent running through the book is food; its preparation, consumption, and enjoyment. The language glows and the story drips with the aromas and flavors of the recipes in the book.

After Breakfast: A trip to the Las Cruces area would not be complete without a visit to White Sands National Monument. The monument offers informative self-guided hikes through beautiful white gypsum dunes where the young at heart can play for hours under blue skies and bask in the hot sun.
www.nps.gov/whsa

International Delights Café

1245 El Paseo Road
Las Cruces, NM 88001
(575) 647-5956
www.
internationaldelightscafe.com

Breakfast Hours:
Monday-Saturday 7am-11am,
Sunday 8am-11am
Kid Component:*
Prices: $$

International Delights Café specializes in Mediterranean and Middle Eastern foods, drinks, and groceries. Breakfast here is truly a delight. We can personally attest to the excellence of six of the seven breakfast items on the menu, and we have been told by those who like lox that the seventh is superb as well.

Breakfast offerings include breakfast combo (choice of bagel, croissant, or toast); egg sandwich (two eggs any style on your choice of bread, served with fruit salad); two egg breakfast (two eggs any style, home fries, fruit salad, and toast); Mediterranean breakfast (omelet filled with kalamata olives and feta cheese, served with warm pita and fruit salad); Middle Eastern breakfast (hummus, falafel, mixed olives, feta cheese); French toast croissant (your choice of strawberry, cherry, or blueberry topping served with fruit salad); and bagel with lox (a plain bagel with smoked salmon, cream cheese, onions, tomatoes, and capers). If you dine at this restaurant before 9am, you will receive a free cup of coffee with your breakfast order.

International Delights also houses a great Middle Eastern grocery store and bakery. You can find rice, olive oil, several kinds of Middle Eastern pastries, and cheeses here; not to mention tea and coffee from around the Mediterranean, Halvah meats, canned vegetables, jams, jellies, and other delicacies not available elsewhere in the area. Free wireless internet and friendly attentive service round out the package.

There is even a fountain and outside patio with chairs and tables (very popular in the summer). Soccer fans can get an added thrill watching their favorite teams on a flat screen HDTV.

This restaurant is a local favorite and should be a "must go" place for a culinary feast.

Recommended Reading: Read about the unsolved 1949 mystery of a murdered waitress in the Las Cruces area in Jason Silverman's *Untold New Mexico: Stories from a Hidden Past*. This book is filled with tantalizing stories from all over the state.

After Breakfast: For a day of outdoor adventure and local history, head to the Dripping Springs/La Cueva Visitors Center, where you will find hiking trails leading you to a former tuberculosis sanatorium, an abandoned hotel, and a hermit's cave.
www.blm.gov/nm/st/en/prog/recreation/las_cruces/dripping_springs.html

Mesilla Valley Kitchen

2001 E. Lohman Ave
Las Cruces, NM 88001
(575) 523-9311

Breakfast Hours:
Monday-Saturday 6am-2:30pm,
Sunday 7am-1:30pm
Kid Component:**
Prices: $

A longtime Las Cruces favorite, the Mesilla Valley Kitchen serves breakfast all day, every day. This eatery is a short jaunt off Interstate 25 and across the street from New Mexico State University. The restaurant is large and often bustling with customers. The menu offers a wide selection of breakfast items with healthy heart options; our favorite being the French toast made with egg whites and served with margarine, delicious butter pecan syrup and a side of fresh fruit.

Huevos rancheros are served with red or green chile and a choice of cheeses plus beans, potatoes, tomatoes, and lettuce. For a hearty breakfast that is guaranteed to last most of the day we recommend the home fries with diced bacon and sausage smothered in red or green chile, cheeses, and a tortilla.

A wide assortment of pancakes includes buttermilk, regular with trail mix sprinkles, pecan pancakes, and Billy cakes with bacon bits mixed into the batter. Eggs any style are carefully prepared and can be ordered separately with toast. Coffee is always served hot and fresh. Teas, juices, milk, and cocoa are very moderately priced.

Customers order at a counter from a big selection posted on the wall as you enter. Sometimes there is a line, but the wait is never too long. This is a terrific spot for meeting friends for a nice visit over coffee and breakfast.

Recommended Reading: *Anything for Billy* by Larry McMurtry may be fiction, but many of the incidents are taken from history. Billy the Kid, renamed Billy Bone in this telling, is probably the most famous and certainly the most notorious New Mexican of the 19th century. Eastern newspapers and their fascination with western outlaws of the period helped Billy's publicity. Yet his story and the characters around him remain the grist for movies, plays, and books well into the 20th and now the 21st century.

After Breakfast: Pecan farms are numerous in the Las Cruces area. Visit Stahmann Farms, one of the largest Pecan farms in the world, located seven miles south of Las Cruces on Highway 28.
www.stahmanns.com

Milaɡro Coffee y Espresso

1733 E. University Ave
Las Cruces, NM 88001
(575) 532-1042

Breakfast Hours: Daily
6:30am-10pm
Kid Component:*
Prices: $

Many locals believe and will proclaim that Milagro Coffee y Espresso offers the best coffee in Las Cruces. The coffee is roasted onsite daily. Pastries, muffins, bagels (with or without cream cheese), and panini sandwiches are available. Cheerful, courteous, knowledgeable service tops off your dining experience in this excellent locally owned coffee house.

An added attraction at this establishment is the fresh squeezed orange juice machine. This drink-making machine is entertaining to watch as the oranges roll down the chute into the grinder. The orange juice produced by this contraption is outstanding. Tempting you away from this orange delight may be the espresso shake. Milagro's has some of the strongest coffee in town and the espresso is a testament to this fact. The espresso shake (espresso combined with vanilla ice cream and whizzed up with milk) is ambrosia that will kick you wide awake clear through the next week.

If you don't have time to come in and sit (a shame, 'cause you're missing an experience), there is a drive-thru window to accommodate you. Space at the tables outside on the covered patio is at a premium in the summer. The owner and staff members are dog friendly, so this is a great place to come with your canine pals. Hummingbird feeders and their visitors are another attraction.

If you are a coffee lover, this is a required stop any time of day.

Recommended Reading: For those interested in the "real wild west," try *Wildest of the Wild West: True Tales of a Frontier Town on the Santa Fe Trail* by Howard Bryan. This is a compilation of articles originally published in the author's "Off the Beaten Path" column in the *Albuquerque Tribune*.

After Breakfast: If you happen to be in town on Wednesday or Sunday, venture over to the Las Cruces Farmers & Craft Market. The market is located in the downtown mall and runs from 8am to noon. At the market you will find a wide variety of local produce and beautiful artwork. www.lascrucescvb.org/html/las_cruces_farmers_and_crafts_.html

Red Mountain Café

1120 Commerce Dr. # A
Las Cruces, NM 88011
(575) 522-7584
www.redmountaincafe.com

Breakfast Hours: Monday-
Saturday 8am-11am,
Sunday 8am-noon
Kid Component:*
Prices: $

Inside or outside, you have a choice of seating at the Red Mountain Café. Casual and comfortable, Red Mountain is the kind of place to meet friends for good food and a long visit. Customers are never rushed and the service is friendly. Breakfast items include ham, bacon, or sausage with eggs; wonderful rosemary potatoes; and pancakes, French toast, omelets, and a foot-long burrito with choice of eighteen different fillings. Side orders are individually priced and the heart-conscious customer can substitute poached eggs. A large fruit salad served with yogurt or cottage cheese and granola will get the healthy hiker on the trail with gusto. Red Mountain Café prepares food in what some call the gourmet style that may satisfy the discriminating taste.

Red Mountain Café was one of the first restaurants in Las Cruces to serve light and tasty meals at breakfast and lunch with specialty coffees. It has become an ideal place to meet friends by plan or surprise.

Recommended Reading: *Following the Royal Road: A Guide to the Historic Camino Real de Tierra Adentro* by Hal Jackson is unique in that it contains aerial and ground photos of sites along the famed trail from its origin in central Mexico to Santa Fe and Taos. For the intrepid traveler, there are maps to show exact locations and names of places that were important to those early Spanish settlers and references to historic events. Whether you can traverse the entire trail or explore a small section, this book provides detailed guidance.

After Breakfast: With the above Recommended Reading in hand, follow the trail traversed by travelers from Mexico, through Las Cruces to Santa Fe. Follow the Royal Road an hour and a half drive north of Las Cruces to the Camino Real International Heritage Center, one of New Mexico's newest museums. At this outstanding and desolate monument you will find an oasis of activity. The museum offers an opportunity to interact with exhibits that tell the story of the people who made the journey through this harsh landscape.

www.caminorealheritage.org

Spirit Winds

2260 Locust St.
Las Cruces, NM 88001
(575) 521-1222
www.spiritwindsçs.
com

Breakfast Hours:
Monday-Friday 7am-7pm,
Saturday 7:30am-7pm,
Sunday 8am-6pm
Kid Component:*
Prices: $

A hangout for students young and old, Spirit Winds offers a cool refuge for anyone seeking enlightenment through food, unusual gifts, and humorous cards. The same light menu is served throughout the day and includes offerings of quiche, freshly baked croissants, scones, bagels, strudel, rolls, muffins, and fresh fruit. All of these dining options are recommended with Spirit Winds' great coffee.

We love to eat here and enjoy free alternative newspapers and unusual art objects on display and for sale. All baked goods are prepared daily on-site with day-old bakery available at a marked down price. The quiche is generous and one of the best in the state. Additional beverages include iced and hot lattes, espressos, teas, Italian sodas, soy milk, juices, and more. Coffee, being one of Spirit Winds specialties, is always freshly made.

Occasionally owner and longtime supporter of the arts, Richard Parra, provides concerts by local musicians outside on the patio. This is the kind of place where you may run into folks you haven't seen for awhile or you may take the opportunity to make new acquaintances.

Spirit Winds is a block from New Mexico State University, convenient to campus, with adequate parking on the premises and nearby. Indoor seating is available and the outdoor seating is cooled with misters during the hot summer months. The extensive gift store opens an hour or so after the restaurant opens its doors and has unique gifts for reasonable prices.

Recommended Reading: *Loving Pedro Infante*, by award-winning author and Las Cruces native Denise Chávez, is about Tere Ávila, a woman as spirited as the winds that buffet New Mexico in the spring. Tere feels trapped by life because she has fallen in love with a married man whose false promises she too often believes. With a sense of humor and the help of her best friend Irma, she tries to tame her longings by watching Pedro Infante movies and having his fan club become a big part of her life in the small dusty desert town of Cabritoville.

After Breakfast: Southern New Mexico is home to some fine wineries. One of our favorites is La Viña Winery in Santa Teresa, about 45 minutes south of Las Cruces. We recommend a back road drive from Las Cruces through La Mesilla. On Hwy 28 you will find La Viña Winery, one of New Mexico's oldest wineries. When planning your visit, be sure to check their website for specific visiting days and hours.
www.lavinawinery.com

Charlie's Bakery and Café

713 Douçlas Avenue
Las Veças, NM 87701
(505) 426-1921

Breakfast Hours:
Monday-Friday 6:30am-6pm
weekdays,
Saturday-Sunday 7am-6pm
Kid Component:***
Prices: $

Charlie's Bakery and Café (formerly the historic "Spic and Span") has been serving Las Vegas since 1950. "The Spic," as it is known locally, started in a small building and was named the Spic and Span because it was so clean. Carmen Cdebaca expanded it during the thirty years she owned it. Charlie Sandoval, the current owner, took over in 1998. This restaurant serves as the meet-and-greet place in Las Vegas, especially on Saturday mornings (when many ranchers in the area come to town) and Sunday mornings after church.

This bakery is known for its fresh-baked goodies, homemade red and green chile, salsa, and tortillas. Those, combined with their use of fresh ingredients, make Charlie's food some of the best in town. Charlie's kitchen makes traditional Northern New Mexican dishes which aren't widely available, and they are always adding new menu items. The beef *empanadas* are made old-style with apples, raisins, and cinnamon. The breakfast *quesadillas* are a new breakfast treat.

Combine fast, friendly service with great food, and you get Charlie's motto: "*Panza Llena Corazon Contento*" (a satisfied belly makes a contented heart). Despite all of the changes, Charlie's is still "Spic and Span" clean.

Recommended Reading: As you sit among the ranchers having breakfast, you might enjoy reading *Old Las Vegas: Hispanic Memories from the New Mexico Meadowlands* collected and translated by Nasario García. García, a former professor at New Mexico Highlands University, has collected these stories in Spanish, with English translations, as a way to preserve an important part of Hispanic culture.

After Breakfast: The railroad arrived in Las Vegas in 1879. Today there are over 900 buildings on the National Register of Historic Places in Las Vegas. The Las Vegas Citizens' Committee for Historic Preservation offers tours and provides self-guided walking information about historic structures. Stop by their office at 127 Bridge Street for information. The historic Carnegie Library will be on the list of historic buildings. The Carnegie building is the only Carnegie library in New Mexico. As you tour Las Vegas, also stop by the Donnelly Library at New Mexico Highlands University.
www.lasvegasnmcchp.com
www.lasvegasnm.gov/library/home.htm
www.nmhu.edu/libraryvenues/hlibrary/index.aspx

Lincoln

Wortley Hotel Dining Room

Highway 380
Lincoln, NM 88338
(575) 653-4300
www.wortleyhotel.com/
page2.html

Breakfast hours:
Tuesday-Sunday 8am-11am
(March-November)
Kid component:**
Price: $$

The roadway through the center of Lincoln has been the stage for raging fights, deadly gunfire, and raucous celebrations. Today, this road (New Mexico Highway 380) runs right in front of the Wortley Hotel Dining Room, a restaurant that has consistently played a supporting role in Lincoln County's historical violence. On one of the town's most historically important days, April 28, 1881, Robert Olinger was in the Wortley Dining Room guarding five prisoners from the courthouse jail, when he heard gunfire coming from across the street. Olinger left the dining room and made his way to the courthouse where Billy the Kid was imprisoned. The Kid had broken free from his guards and gained possession of a gun. As Olinger approached the courthouse, Billy shot and killed him and then escaped town on horseback.

As exciting as history has been in Lincoln, today you will find a serene small town with less than 75 full-time residents. The Wortley Hotel and its dining room provide a stage for vacations filled with peace and quiet.

The Wortley Hotel was purchased by Vic and Cathy Garrison in 2007. Vic prepares breakfast at the hotel, and Cathy brings it to your table with a genuine smile. The couple has restored the hotel to luxurious comfort. Guestrooms are comfortably appointed with antique marble-topped dressers and brass beds. The guestrooms are free of telephones and televisions (WiFi is available), encouraging guests to filter out on to the wide wooden porch for an afternoon of reading and an evening of conversation with guests and Lincoln locals.

The Wortley Dining Room is a light-filled room with wooden chairs and tables. Guests staying overnight at the Wortley Hotel will have their breakfasts included with the price of their room. Breakfast in the dining room is a true treat. Just walking in the door, your imagination allows you to smell rich syrup drizzled over 100 years of pancakes, and listening carefully you might hear the historic snapping of bacon and sizzling potatoes.

The breakfast menu is brief but filled with all the breakfast options you would expect. We were told on a recent visit that the *migas* (eggs served over crispy tortillas) are a local favorite, and people drive from miles around to enjoy this breakfast item. The *huevos rancheros* are also a fine breakfast selection, as are the blueberry pancakes. Every dish is made with fresh ingredients and attention to detail. All of the breakfast entrées are served with wonderful coffee, orange juice, or tea.

The Wortley Hotel Dining Room provides great food and a restful place to pause, restore, and begin a day full of adventure.

Recommended Reading: Have all of your Lincoln history questions answered by reading William A. Keleher's *Violence in Lincoln County 1869-1881* (in a New Edition from Sunstone Press).

After Breakfast: The entire town of Lincoln has played an important role in New Mexico's Wild West history. After breakfast, step out of the dining room and right into history. Walk to the museum or the courthouse and buy a ticket to view the entire Lincoln State Monument, which includes seventeen structures.
www.nmmonuments.org/inst.php?inst=7

Los Alamos

Hot Rocks Java Café

4200 West Jemez Road
Suite 203
Los Alamos, NM
(505) 663-5282

Breakfast hours: Monday-
Friday 6am-11am
Kid Component:*
Prices: $

Across the street from the Los Alamos National Laboratory (LANL) Research Library, and beside the Fire Station, is a modern three story building called The Research Park. (Hint for finding the building: look for the huge letters UCSD on the south side of the building and UCSB on the east side). On the main floor of the Research Park is a small café called Hot Rocks.

Don't let the stealth appearance deter you. The mystique of the LANL classified work area has seeped into this building; there is no sign for this restaurant, but the comfortable outdoor seating will indicate that food and coffee are to be found nearby. Directly behind the outdoor tables and seating is the door to Hot Rocks, a locally owned and operated café. The "made from scratch" food, free Wi-Fi, and zany customers make this a lively spot.

Hot Rocks attracts a unique set of patrons from Los Alamos National Laboratory. Many scientists come from a tradition of coffeehouses in their hometowns in Europe, Asia, or South America; and seem to be at home in this hidden locale. The conversational buzz is created from an array of languages and accents. At Hot Rocks, you'll be surrounded by the language of science, not the conversation of tourists.

Because of the Euro customers, espressos are served in appropriate china. Coffee is available along with Italian sodas, Belgium chocolates, and, of course, Northern New Mexico chile. Local New Mexican dishes vie with quiche and panini specials.

The cozy room is furnished for a constant re-arrangement of tables and chairs as teams and friends arrive to work and eat at this café. The periphery has small tables usually occupied by singles with laptops. As you might imagine, the café can be crowded at lunch and during work breaks; but the overflow of customers is easily accommodated by fast turnover and outdoor seating in the summer.

At Hot Rocks everything is fresh, fresh, fresh. Every order is hand-built by a team of athletic chefs that can be viewed in their running shoes and shorts cooking non-stop and at high speed in the immaculate kitchen.

The stream of LANL scientists and staff order coffee, breakfast burritos, omelets, scones, and seasonal fruit/yogurt mixes.

Recommended Reading: Read about early beginnings of Los Alamos in Jennet Conant's *190 East Palace: Robert Oppenheimer and the Secret City of Los Alamos.* Conant's book reveals the lives of the ordinary people who were asked to think and live in extraordinary ways during World War II. Everyone assigned to Los Alamos crossed a literal and historic threshold at 190 East Palace in Santa Fe.

After Breakfast: Head to the nearby Los Alamos National Laboratory Research Library for a unique history lesson. On permanent display on the main level of the library's Study Center is a quilt with 58 squares representing the symbols, scenery, and structures so unique to Los Alamos. Created in 1981 by the Pajarito Chapter of the Embroidery Guild of America, the quilt was made to honor the town's 40th anniversary and presented to the LANL Research Library. And speaking of quilts, a visit to Mesa Public Library in historic "downtown" Los Alamos would not be complete without seeing the fabulous handmade quilts featuring beloved characters from children's literature visible from the curved stairway leading down to the children's room.
www.library.lanl.gov
www.library.losalamosnm.us

Charlie's Restaurant/Price's Truck Stop

5406 Main St N
Roswell, NM 88201
(575) 623-3443

Breakfast Hours:
Daily 5am-10pm; Breakfast
Buffet Daily 5:00am-11am
Kid Component:***
Price: $

Expect to see a variety of vehicles at Charlie's Restaurant at Price's truck stop—18-wheelers, 5th wheelers, assorted horse trailers, pick-ups, and cars. There might be an array of two-wheeled modes of transportation, mainly motorcycles. And given Roswell's history, you might even spot some flying saucers in or over the parking lot on the far north end of Main Street.

Truth be told, on our visits we've never seen any aliens among the cowboys, truckers, bikers, tourists, and local folks who occupy the booths, tables, and seats at the counter in this spacious yet homey establishment. Everyone seems to come here for close encounters of the food kind. And the only real flying saucers are likely to be those under the cups of hot coffee that come sailing out of the kitchen in the hands of your efficient waitress.

Long haul ahead? Steak (rib eye or chicken-fried), pork chops, and the Trucker's Special (three eggs, bacon, ham, and sausage plus toast and hash browns) should hold you until the next station (service, weigh, inspection, or space). Mexican breakfast items include a burrito and *huevos rancheros,* plus the Santa Fe Scramble: eggs, onions, ham, green chile, tomatoes, and cheese served over hash browns with a flour tortilla. Several kinds of omelets come with hash browns and your choice of toast, while the pancakes, waffles, and French toast promise your choice of syrups. The breakfast menu is extensive and all items are available all day.

No matter what day you land in Roswell, Charlie's Breakfast Buffet is out of this world, at a down to earth price. Any morning from 5:00 to 11am you can mix and match pancakes, waffles, French toast, bacon, sausage eggs, potatoes, biscuits, gravy, fruit, cereal, and juice.

"American food at its homemade best since 1955" is the slogan on the front of the menu. Portions are generous, so if someone yells "Where's the beef?" don't worry. They're no doubt referring to the giant bovine on wheels out in front of the restaurant. This sign, doubling as a parade float, is no doubt visible from space or at least from the nearby intersection of Highways 287 and 75.

Recommended Reading: Roswell had a space connection long before the famous "UFO Incident" of 1947. Former Chief Historian of the U.S. Forest Service and Roswell resident David A. Clary is the author of *Rocket Man: The Life and Legends of Robert H. Goddard, American Pioneer of Space Flight.*

After Breakfast: Goddard's workshop has been recreated as part of the Collection of Liquid-Propellant Rocketry at the Roswell Museum and Art Center. Mounted on the roof's edge, letters spelling out the names of famous authors (including New Mexico's own Hillerman and Anaya), cast interesting shadows on the outside walls of the Roswell Public Library. The Roswell UFO Festival is held annually around the 4th of July weekend. To spot *Identified* Flying Objects, visit the Bitter Lake National Wildlife Refuge, which supports one of the most diverse populations of dragonflies and damselflies in North America. Over 90 species reside here, including the continent's largest and smallest dragonfly species.
www.roswellpubliclibrary.org
www.fws.gov/southwest/refuges/newmex/bitterlake/index.html

Ruidoso Downs

Jorge's Café

2064 Hwy 70W
Ruidoso Downs, NM 88346
(575) 378-9804

Breakfast Hours:
Daily 7am-10am
Kid Component:**
Prices: $

If you find yourself in the village of Ruidoso Downs on Highway 70, breakfast at Jorge's Café is a must. Tourists in town for skiing, horse racing, casino visits, or shopping sometimes discover this homey family-owned café, but many of the regulars at this eatery are local folks from Ruidoso and Ruidoso Downs who know good food when they taste it.

This small café offers seating at ten tables and seven booths. The décor is eclectic, the atmosphere is casual, and the view from the front windows will remind you that you are in the mountains.

The blending of Mexican and American cultures is evident in the menu. Daily breakfast specials are available in addition to egg plates, meat plates, and "South of the Border" favorites. For diners with large appetites, Jorge's breakfast meat plates feature sirloin steaks, rib eyes, chicken-fried steaks, and pork chops. The omelets are enormous and tasty. The burritos smothered in green chile are mouth-watering good. For those interested in less meat-intensive entrées, the big breakfast contains two eggs, two pieces of bacon, two sausages, ham, hash browns, and two pancakes.

Other offerings on the menu include pancakes, waffles, and

French toast. "South of the Border" breakfast favorites include *menudo*, *huevos rancheros*, and *huevos con chorizo* or *machaca*. The *chilaquiles* plate, a tasty combination of tortilla chips, eggs, and red chile with a side of beans, is *delicioso*!

Recommended Reading: The red chile sauce in the *chilaquiles* brings to mind *Chiles for Benito/Chiles para Benito*, a bilingual (English-Spanish) picture book by Ana Baca that tells a magical story of New Mexican chiles and ristras. The book also contains a recipe for red chile sauce for those who wish to prepare their own.

After Breakfast: Head over to the stunning Hubbard Museum of the American West. The museum offers an ever-changing menu of exhibits along with beautiful sculptures of horses. This is a first-class museum you can visit again and again, and see something new on every visit. www.hubbardmuseum.org

San Antonio

Acosta's Mexican Restaurant

15 South Pino
San Antonio, NM 87832
(575) 835-1688

Breakfast Hours:
Daily 7am-2pm
Kid Component:**
Prices: $

San Antonio is best known for its proximity to Bosque del Apache National Wildlife Refuge along the central Rio Grande. In fall and winter months, many thousands of sandhill cranes, snow geese, and other migrating waterfowl dwell at "the Bosque," thrilling locals and visitors from dawn until dark with their aerial/riparian lifestyles.

After bird-watching from pre-dawn to well past sunrise at the wintry Bosque, there is no better warm-up than breakfast at Acosta's Mexican Restaurant, back up the road in San Antonio. The *huevos rancheros*, breakfast *enchiladas*, *carne adovada*, and ubiquitous burritos are all top-flight.

Matriarch Maria Acosta built her little restaurant six years ago in the heart of the village. She opened propitiously on the Feast of Saint Anthony (San Antonio) and, as the family will attest, the blessings have never ceased. Doña Maria learned 'the biz' working for years with the late Manny Olguin at the famous Buckhorn Bar next door.

Maria has retired and her daughters and granddaughters now run Acosta's. The ambiance is simple but intimate. In warmer months patio seating is available.

Recommended Reading: Pigeons' (doves') plaintive cooing sings the sun up and back down each day on the desert. These birds will serenade you at Acosta's. But you've never known pigeons until you've read *Aloft: A Meditation on Pigeons and Pigeon-Flying*, by New Mexico author and outdoorsman Stephen Bodio.

After Breakfast: Plan a trip to the Bosque Del Apache Wildlife Refuge. The refuge is a stopping place for thousands of migrating birds and is home to mammals year-round.
www.fws.gov/southwest/refuges/newmex/bosque/index.html

Santa Fe Area

Café Paris

31 Burro Alley
Santa Fe, NM 87501
(505) 986-9162
www.cafeparisnm.com

Breakfast hours:
Daily 8am-11:30am
Kid Component:*
Prices: $$

You'll feel like an American in Paris at this charming café, or as it says right over the door, "a true Montmartre bistro." To eat here, you won't need a passport or even a French dictionary! Cleverly hidden in historic Burro Alley, just a *promenade* from the Plaza, a person might not even notice the Café Paris unless the weather happens to be warm enough for the outside tables and umbrellas to be set up in the street. But you don't have to be Hercule Poirot to find this place, once you decide to investigate the source of the enticing aromas wafting out the door.

Don't resist the impulse to walk up to the display of fresh homemade pastries. Brioches, croissants, (plain, almond, or chocolate), raisin rolls, palmiers, lemon tarts, raspberry scones, and a bounty of beautiful cookies are artistically arranged. Maybe you'll want to take some of these delights with you when you leave.

Meanwhile, it's time for *le petit-déjeuner.* There are six omelets to choose from. Although we strive to sample a variety of menu items on our visits, the omelet lyonnaise always ends up in front of one of us. It contains a superb combination of sautéed onion and bacon, and is topped with lusciously melting shredded Swiss cheese. If you're not exactly *la vie en rose* type, but instead prefer *la vie en chile,* then the *chorizo* or *chipotle* omelets are your style. All omelets are served with sautéed garlic potatoes and toasted bread. Lovers of poached eggs are not forgotten at the Café Paris; say *bonjour* to eggs Benedict and Florentine.

Feeling like some dessert to add *joie de vivre* to breakfast? The repertoire includes crème brulée, chocolate mousse, profiterole, apple tatin, tiramisu, café liegeois, mamadou, napoleon, black forest cake, and California tart.

Weather permitting, dine *alfresco.* Outside, tables are covered with flowery yellow oilcloth. Large green umbrellas provide shade. Take time to admire the huge mosaic on the wall of the building facing the café. It memorializes the Lensic Theater (now the Lensic Performing Arts Center), a Santa Fe landmark right around the corner on San Francisco Street.

The café's interior affords more than a *soupçon* of French flavor. Murals on the walls and ceilings portray Notre Dame cathedral, the Eiffel Tower, Montmartre, the Moulin Rouge, and the Seine, plus scenes of the can-can and Parisians being Parisians. *Naturellement,* there are framed Lautrec and Mucha posters.

Recommended Reading: We bet you're feeling guilty for choosing that apple tart for breakfast, *n'est-ce pas*? Let us recommend *French Women Don't Get Fat: The Secret of Eating for Pleasure* by Mireille Guiliano. Take two chocolate croissants and call us in the morning.

After Breakfast: The ambience of Café Paris may make you hungry for great art. The Georgia O'Keeffe Museum is less than two blocks away. www.okeeffemuseum.org

Café Pasqual's

121 Don Gaspar
Santa Fe, NM 87501
(505) 983-9340
(800) 722-7672
www.pasquals.com

Breakfast Hours:
Daily 8am-3pm
Kid Component: *
Prices: $$

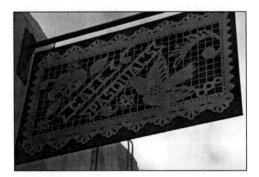

Have you ever wondered what it would be like to be in the eye of a hurricane? How about in the eye of a *fiesta*? Welcome to Hurricane Pasqual—make that Café Pasqual's. Don't worry; you won't be blown away, except maybe by the incredible food, which has been served here for over 28 years.

Since the restaurant's official capacity is 49 patrons (according to the sign near the door), be prepared to wait for seating. Should you need some reading material to pass the time, elbow your way to the cash register and purchase a copy of the *Café Pasqual's Cookbook* (subtitled *Spirited Recipes from Santa Fe)*. If you arrive early, ask for a table on the upper level near the window. This will give you an excellent view of the wall murals by the renowned Mexican painter Leovigildo Martinez, depicting the moon reveling at her fiesta. Rows and rows of *papel picado*, intricately cut tissue paper banners, flutter above you from the ceiling.

One of our favorite dishes of all time is at this restaurant: Pasqual's version of the breakfast quesadilla. This luscious entrée includes perfectly prepared scrambled eggs, cheese, and the best breakfast guacamole you may ever experience. This is all sandwiched between griddled wheat tortillas, and served with a side of gourmet salsa.

One of our frequent breakfast companions hardly ever wavers from the smoked trout hash (golden hash brown potatoes topped with two poached eggs, and a "scatter" of smoked trout, served with *tomatillo chile d'arbol salsa*). However, he has been known to order the *huevos motuleños*—(Yucatan-style eggs over easy on corn tortillas with black beans topped with sautéed bananas, feta cheese, green peas and salsa fresca, served with green chile or tomatillo salsa). Bananas for breakfast? Sounds like just the dish for *Jorge el Curioso*. Jorge would probably also love *tamal dulce* (sweet corn and raisin tamal wrapped in banana leaves, served with black beans, half mango, and Mexican hot chocolate).

Pasqual's uses only natural and organic ingredients, including organic eggs and naturally raised beef and pork. The sausage and *chorizo* are made on the premises. There's nary a pink, blue, or yellow packet of artificial sweetener in sight. Instead you'll find packs of Xylitol (all-natural wood sugar) or honey.

There are several small tables on both levels, plus one booth. If you happen to be dining alone, or your party doesn't require the intimacy of its own table (and you enjoy serendipitous happenings), join the large "community table." It seats 10, and is ideal for general discussions and the sharing of information among strangers.

A woman across from us at the community table, who had ordered the fried blue and yellow cornmeal mush, asked the server where she could purchase blue cornmeal to take home to New Jersey, and mentioned she was also looking for blue corn hominy. Since we had recently been to the Farmers Market and seen blue hominy for sale at a booth there, we felt comfortable chiming in with this valuable piece of information.

Recommended Reading: To decorate your own ceiling, Café Pasqual's style, consult *Making Magic Windows: Creating Papel Picado/ Cut-Paper Art* by Carmen Lomas Garza.

After Breakfast: It's a short stroll up to the Plaza, the heart of Santa Fe. The Palace of the Governors faces one side, and the Cathedral Basilica of St. Francis of Assisi, built by Archbishop Jean Baptiste Lamy, is just one block further.
www.palaceofthegovernors.org
www.cbsfa.org

Flying Tortilla

4250-D Cerrillos Road
(505) 424-1680
www.flyingtortilla.com/

Breakfast Hours:
Daily 6:30am-3pm
Kid Component: *
Prices: $

It's a bird, it's a plane...no it's a flying tortilla! Flying tortillas bring to mind many imaginative visions: tortillas with snow white wings, tortillas flung across the table in the heat of a grand debate, tortilla dough spinning through the air before landing on a hot cook top. The staff at this restaurant actually assured us that no tortillas have flown in the restaurant, but the thought of going to the Flying Tortilla for breakfast in the morning may get you flying out of bed.

This restaurant is large and spacious and almost always hopping with activity. On a recent midweek visit we spent nearly two hours chatting and enjoying our breakfast amid the hustle and bustle. Our coffee cups were never empty while we watched National Guard personnel dine on giant omelets, pancakes, and French toast; a woman escort her elderly father to a table and enjoy hot tea, corned beef, and eggs; and a construction worker sit alone at the community table to eat a breakfast burrito.

We also enjoyed the breakfast burrito with the Egg Beaters option, served with the same excellent red chile flavored potatoes. One of our dining companions designed her own breakfast sandwich which included scrambled eggs, bacon, and cheese all wrapped in a low carb tortilla.

The Flying Tortilla is a great place for large family group meals or meetings with coworkers. The front of the restaurant is devoted to a separate dining space that can be closed off from restaurant's main room, allowing for private family banter and lively collegial discussions.

The Flying Tortilla's location on the south side of Santa Fe allows Albuquerque drivers easy access to great food on the way in to town. Commuters will not be disappointed with any of these meals picked up on-the-go.

Recommended Reading: In *The Runaway Tortilla* by Eric A. Kimmel, a tortilla runs away from a woman who is about to cook him. A southwestern version of *The Gingerbread Man*, here the tortilla is chased by Tía Lupe and Tío José, two horned toads, three donkeys, four jackrabbits, five rattlesnakes, and six buckaroos.

After Breakfast: Take advantage of being on the south side of Santa Fe by visiting the Santa Fe Public Library's beautiful Southside Branch at 6599 Jaguar Drive.
www.santafelibrary.org

Guadalupe Café

422 Old Santa Fe Trail
Santa Fe, NM 87501
(505) 982-9762

Breakfast Hours:
Tuesday-Friday 8am-11am,
Saturday-Sunday 8am-2pm
Kid Component:*
Prices: $$

Guadalupe Café is a lovely, very quaint adobe with potted fresh flowers, interesting artwork, and cozy little rooms. The building's white stucco is cheerful with plenty of light, and the outside patio overlooks Old Santa Fe Trail. Inside, there's a nice fireplace to snuggle near when the weather is chilly. Centrally located between the State Capitol Building (the Roundhouse) and the Plaza, the café is a convenient oasis for visitors exploring this historic area. The restaurant was originally located on Guadalupe Street, but a need for more space led to the move to its present location. Parking is available behind the restaurant.

The New Mexican cuisine at the café is "to die for," with generous portions served at a very moderate price. A shared birthday was the occasion for a recent Sunday brunch with another couple. Since the Guadalupe Café does not take reservations, our friends rightly decided to arrive early, securing a table, otherwise we might have had quite a wait. Each member of the party ordered something different on the varied menu, and we all agreed that everything was wonderful.

A burrito, creatively prepared with an egg, mushroom, and spinach filling, was very fresh tasting and the spinach inside was not overcooked. A tasty (and huge) omelet received rave reviews. Toasted cinnamon bread and poppy seed muffins ensured that we wouldn't need more than a light dinner that evening. All of us were impressed with the quality of the food, size of the portions, and reasonable prices.

We recommend ordering your chile "Christmas" (part red, part green) so you can sample both the wonderful sauces. We have never felt rushed dining at the Guadalupe Café, and the wait staff is attentive even during the restaurant's busiest times.

Recommended Reading: Children (with adult supervision) will enjoy trying the many fun recipes in *Cody Coyote Cooks!: A Southwest Cookbook For Kids* by Denice Skrepcinski, Melissa T. Stock, and Lois Bergthold. The book includes recipes for corn and flour tortillas made from scratch. Additionally, there is a small section for crafts such as cornhusk dolls. (Cornhusks: they're not just for tamales any more!)

After Breakfast: Visit the New Mexico State Capitol Building next door to the Guadalupe Café. Art critics have claimed the Capitol collection of art is the best collection of New Mexico's contemporary art available to the public. The art may be viewed any time the Capitol is open. While visiting, don't miss the Governor's Gallery on the 4th floor where six rotating exhibits are curated every year.
www.collectorsguide.com/sf/sffa10.shtml

Harry's Roadhouse

96 Old Las Veças
Hiçhway
Santa Fe, NM 87505
(505) 989-4629

Breakfast Hours: Monday-
Friday 7am-11am,
Saturday 7am-noon,
Sunday 7am-1pm
Kid Component:***
Prices: $$

Harry's Roadhouse sits cozily in the eastern foothills of Santa Fe on the Old Las Vegas Highway; a road that serves as a frontage road to Interstate 25. On a weekend visit to Harry's Roadhouse you may notice from quite a distance cars, trucks, motorcycles, bicycles, and people on foot streaming into Harry's parking lot. This restaurant is a local favorite and on the "must experience" list for many visitors to Santa Fe.

Opening the front door, you will be warmly greeted by a host or hostess. The staff at Harry's is filled with people who enjoy their jobs, making for a terrific dining experience no matter how early you cross the threshold.

If the restaurant isn't too full, you may be offered a choice of seating options. Each room will garner a slightly different dining experience. The dining room in the bar area is a warm space with small intimate café tables. The dining area to the right of the front door is a room that might have been pulled out of a 1950s diner and placed into this roadside café. The middle room in the restaurant is filled with large bright-colored tables and serves as an art gallery. In warmer months the back patio and outside dining areas are terrific options.

The menu at Harry's Roadhouse is outstanding, and the "Breakfast Specials" menu is not to be ignored. The ever-changing menu at some restaurants may be disconcerting, but when you eat at Harry's, you can rest assured that everything on the menu is good, and even while an old favorite may disappear, there are at least twenty other mouthwatering options from which to choose.

Despite seasonal changes to the menu, the breakfast burrito is always available, with a side of potatoes. Bagels, an assortment of pancakes and waffles, and other more traditional spicy breakfast dishes are available daily. We can recommend the lemon ricotta pancakes topped with fresh strawberries and powdered sugar. The lemon is so rich and subtle that these cakes can easily be eaten without butter or syrup. Eating this sweet treat for breakfast will cause your head to buzz with the joy of sweet sugar.

We also really enjoyed the *migas* (scrambled eggs with peppers, tomatoes, onions, and crispy blue corn tortilla strips) served with a side of salsa, black beans, and a tortilla. This spicy breakfast is filling. Having *migas* or a breakfast burrito with "Peyton's Great Cinnamon Roll" creates the perfect sweet and hearty breakfast meal.

Eating at Harry's you will find a great mix of Santa Fe's residents and visitors. Young intellectuals discuss philosophy, a retired couple reviews a road map, middle-aged motorcycle riders read the local newspaper, and families with five children under 10 years old gracefully balance their lives.

Recommended Reading: Sitting in Harry's watching New Mexico's characters saunter in and out the front door, you might wonder if Jack Kerouac would have stopped in this roadhouse as he crisscrossed the southwest. Jack Kerouac's *On the Road* is classic reading for this classic restaurant.

After Breakfast: Head into the Sangre de Cristo Mountains and take one of several trails. We recommend the Atalaya Mountain trail with a trailhead at St. John's College.
www.sdcmountainworks.com/hiking/trails.php

Horseman's Haven Café

4354 Cerrillos Road
(505) 471-5420

Breakfast Hours: Monday-
Saturday 8am-8pm,
Sunday 8:30am-2pm
Kid Component: **
Prices: $

When the waitress says "red or green?" and follows up right away with "The green is hotter"...*trust her!* Especially if you're not fully awake.

Horseman's Haven's breakfast burrito (two scrambled eggs, two strips of bacon topped with chile and melted cheese, served with home fries) is a classic. Smothered with red, it's plenty hot. You'd think the Fire Marshall would put a ban on anything hotter, considering the restaurant's location so close to a gas station. Okay, you might not actually see the Fire Marshall here, but if the parking lot is any indication, the place seems to be a favorite of the State Police (and it's probably not just because their headquarters are just down the street).

A sure-fire (sorry, couldn't resist) indicator of perfection in the hotness of chile is the need for tissues. If your eyes water after the first couple bites, and you're wiping away tears of joy...that's perfection, and it's here. Perfection of another kind can be experienced in the Horseman's Haven's home fries. They're made of pure potatoes (no onion, bacon, chile, nothing but spuds!) with the exact amount of butter flavor to deliver yet another taste bud triumph.

Horseman's Haven rounds up the usual suspects for breakfast: *huevos rancheros*, omelets, pancakes, French toast, *carne adovada*, *chorizo*, steak and eggs, and so forth. As it says right at the top of the menu, "Bienvenidos: New Mexican style cooking—Como en su casa." If people cooked this well at home, this place wouldn't be nearly as packed as it is.

Then there's the décor. It's a haven for horsemen all right, from the paintings of cowboys in action to the long horns mounted over the window between the counter and the kitchen. Naturally there are portraits of John Wayne, plus a reproduction of the movie poster for "Hondo," starring The Duke. A ristra of red, green, yellow, and purple chile lights twinkles on one wall.

The stools at the counter can accommodate several people, otherwise booths and tables are available. In addition, there are two massive curved corner banquettes providing spacious yet cozy areas for groups of six or so. The 8:00am opening (8:30 on Sunday) is a drawback for early birds and folks wanting to swing by on the way to work. Once the place is open, though, the restaurant bursts with people. Breakfast is available all day, although pancakes and French toast are only served until 11am. And there's takeout, too!

Yet another phrase found on the menu is "Ojala! You enjoy your comida" which loosely translates to "Here's hoping/let's hope you enjoy your meal." The cooks and staff seem eager to make sure that happens.

Recommended Reading: Buster Burro thinks that men wear bandana scarves in order to keep their whiskers out of their beans in Tony Hillerman's kid-friendly *Buster Mesquite's Cowboy Band*, illustrated by Ernest Franklin.

After Breakfast: Head down Cerrillos Road and link up with Interstate 25 going south. Take exit 276 for El Rancho de los Golondrinas, a living history museum dedicated to the heritage and culture of Spanish Colonial New Mexico. Open only part of the year; find details on the website's calendar of events.
www.golondrinas.org

Lamy Station Café

150 Old Lamy Trail
Lamy, NM, 87540
(505) 466-1904
www.lamystationcafe.com

Breakfast hours:
Saturday 8:30am-3pm,
Sunday 10am-3pm
Kid component:*
Price: $$

Dining at this restaurant is a true historic adventure. The Lamy Station Café is located in a restored dining car next to the Lamy Depot. Walking up the stairs to this restaurant, you may hear the wind carry the ghostly bellow of a conductor hollering, "All aboard!" Stepping inside this stand-alone dining car, the sights and sounds may inspire excitement as you dream of train traveling adventures.

The Lamy Station Café finds its home in the historic "Talladega" car. This is an authentic 1950s Pullman dining car that ushered people in luxury on the rails through the 1970s. The car was owned by the Atlantic Coastline Railroad, a railroad that ran in the southern and eastern parts of the United States. The dining car was purchased in 2004 and was brought to New Mexico from Hudson, Colorado in an effort to build the Lamy Railroad and History Museum. The car was cleaned, repaired, and restored by Sam Latkin, Allan Anderson, and Chef Michael Gintert (the man who will make your meal in the renovated kitchen housed in the east end of the dining car).

The inside of the dining car has been refurbished, but its historic seating arrangements have not been altered since it hosted railroad travelers in the middle of the last century. Small seats and 12 tables line the dining car walls. Tables are available for parties of two and parties of four. Small square windows line the car providing picturesque views of the foothills that surround Lamy. The experience of sitting in a dining car and looking out the windows is so thrilling you might even feel the gentle tug of an old train engine pulling you to a distant destination.

Chef Michael is a wonderful chef, so coming to the Lamy Station is worth the drive for the food alone, but it is easy to be distracted by the experience of sitting in an historic railroad car.

We highly recommend the *huevos rancheros* served with pinto beans or potatoes and a tortilla on the side. You might also coordinate your breakfast with the railroad theme and try the "Conductor," a dish that comes with your choice of eggs, bacon or sausage, potatoes, and toast or a tortilla. Omelets, biscuits and gravy, and French toast are all recommended options. The wait staff is attentive and will be around to fill your coffee several times, even on a short trip.

Recommended Reading: Read all about the railroad's influence on Santa Fe's tourism in Victoria E. Dye's book *All Aboard for Santa Fe: Railway Promotion of the Southwest, 1890s to 1930s.*

After Breakfast: The Lamy Depot has served as the entrance to Santa Fe for many train passengers. Take some time to walk around the California mission-style depot right next door to the diner. The depot is in daily operation, serving passengers traveling on Amtrak.

Pantry Restaurant

1820 Cerrillos Road
Santa Fe, NM 87505
(505) 986-0022
www.santafestation.com/
pantry/index.html

Breakfast Hours:
6:30am-2:30pm
Kid Component: ***
Price: $$

The Pantry Restaurant is a long-time favorite of Santa Feans and a wonderful casual dining option for visitors who want to have a real local breakfast experience. 2008 marked the Pantry's 60th anniversary, and that event is commemorated on the cups, boasting "Santa Fe's meeting place since 1948."

There are distinct dining areas in the restaurant. If you are eating alone or in need of a quick bite, stake out a stool at the counter and watch wait staff pick up the food that pours out of the kitchen. The front room of the Pantry has café tables. The best seat in the house is a table-for-two in front of the building's main window, affording a clear view of the busy traffic on Cerrillos Road. Most of the seating is in the back room, where you will find a giant mural on the south wall artfully depicting New Mexico's history and geography. If you have children along, you will probably feel most comfortable in this spacious room.

No matter where you sit, this restaurant is known for its great breakfasts. Our favorite entrée is the breakfast burrito with bacon and red or green chile. Most breakfasts are served with perfectly seasoned red chile potatoes (Pantry fries) and pinto beans. A smaller version of the burrito is the breakfast sandwich with the same ingredients as its big brother but in a single fold of a tortilla. Yet another spicy breakfast specialty is *huevos consuelo* (eggs on a corn tortilla smothered with a tasty sauce). The sweet breakfasts are highly recommended. The stuffed pancakes are folded and filled with fresh mouthwatering blueberries or strawberries. The Belgian waffle is also a favorite. Both sweet breakfasts include real whipped cream that perfectly balances the fruit.

If you find yourself at the Pantry on a weekend morning, be prepared for a wait. There is plenty of outdoor seating where you can watch cars and pedestrians on Santa Fe's main thoroughfare, but be sure to bundle up if visiting during the winter months. Eating at the Pantry is always worth the wait. We have dined here over 30 times in the last six years and consistently find great service and wonderful food.

Before leaving, be sure to take a close look at the framed movie poster, Heart of the Golden West, featuring Roy Rogers and Trigger that hangs on the wall by the end of the lunch counter. Also admire the quilt over the fireplace that depicts the restaurant. If you've been dining with children, you'll recognize the design. It appears on the placemat that the youngsters received (along with crayons) when they were seated.

Recommended Reading: In her book, *Only in Santa Fe*, Denise Kusel writes, "When I wrote my first check for $2.56 for a breakfast in a place where most people spoke Spanglish and the chile was hot enough to spring new tears to my eyes, I knew I had arrived in a place that mattered."

After Breakfast: The Santa Fe Farmers Market is nationally famous. Located at 1607 Paseo de Peralta, the days and hours of operation vary depending on the time of year.
www.santafefarmersmarket.com/

Real Burçer

2239 Old Pecos Trail
Santa Fe, NM 87505
(505) 820-3311

Breakfast hours:

Tuesday-Sunday 7am-11am
Kid component:***
Price: $$

Real Burger is a restaurant full of pleasant surprises and quirky contradictions. For example, most of us would not consider going to a restaurant called Real Burger for breakfast, but think again; this is a premier stop for breakfast in Santa Fe. If you come to Real Burger thinking you might have a burger for breakfast, you will have to reconsider your options because burgers are not even on the menu for breakfast! Does the restaurant name, Real Burger, bring to mind a 1950s style restaurant? If so, you will have to reconsider that idea, too. Real Burger is an upscale diner with excellent service and equally excellent food for breakfast.

Real Burger is located on the edge of Santa Fe, on Old Pecos Trail, only a couple of miles off the Interstate. It is an easy restaurant to visit if you are driving through Santa Fe on your way to northern or southern locales. It is also the perfect off-the-beaten-path restaurant for those of you who have grown weary of finding parking and fighting crowds on the Plaza or Cerrillos Road. There is plenty of parking, and never a wait for a breakfast table at this restaurant.

Large windows, giant booths, and café tables are just some of the features you will notice as you are seated. Red walls and a corrugated metal ceiling punctuate the restaurant's décor. This comfortable restaurant hums with conversation all morning.

The meal starts off with wonderful hot coffee served by dedicated staff who will quickly take your order. Just as you are relaxing with your morning drink and newly opened newspaper, your breakfast order will arrive from the kitchen on plates filled with large portions of steaming fresh food.

We highly recommend the breakfast burrito, an entrée you can order smothered with chile or in a hand-held version. Breakfast burritos are served with your choice of bacon, sausage, ham, *chorizo*, *chicharrones*, or *carne adovada* (we love the *chorizo* and *carne adovada* options). On a recent visit we also fell in love with the *huevos adovada*, an entrée with eggs served atop a generous tender portion of *carne adovada*. Providing a nice balance to the spicy, meaty breakfast, the *huevos adovada* came with a unique but simple side dish: a corn tortilla, topped with potatoes and cheese.

If eggs are not your favorite breakfast treat, try one of Real Burger's fruit-topped pancake or waffle entrées. French toast and oatmeal are also available.

Real Burger has operated in several locations in Santa Fe since its original opening in 1974. We think Real Burger has found a real home serving really good food in this fantastic Old Pecos Trail location.

Recommended Reading: In Julia Glass' novel, *The Whole World Over*, Greenie Duquette moves from New York City to Santa Fe to work as a personal chef for New Mexico's gregarious governor. Santa Fe culture becomes the backdrop in Greenie's journey toward self-discovery.

After Breakfast: Santa Fe's Museum Hill is just a hop, skip, and a jump from Real Burger. Museum Hill is home to the Museum of Spanish Colonial Art, Museum of Indian Arts & Culture, Museum of International Folk Art, and the Wheelwright Museum of the American Indian. museumhill.org/explore.php

San Marcos Café

3877 State Road 14
Santa Fe, NM 87508
(505) 471-9298

Breakfast Hours:
Daily 8am-2pm
Kid Component:**
Prices: $$

For over twenty-five years, San Marcos Café has combined a cozy, eclectic atmosphere with delicious food. About twenty minutes south of Santa Fe, the café is a bright and lively spot frequented by locals and food aficionados. As you head down Highway 14, look for the "Café Open" sign, a large red abstract sculpture, and two life-size cut-outs of cows.

The décor is country/New Mexican with brightly colored, hand painted chairs, a fascinating old stove, an upright radio, knickknacks from around the world, and photos of the café's peacocks. If possible, request a seat in the side room where you will find a kiva fireplace and a view of live peacocks, turkeys, and chickens which roam freely outside.

The strutting birds are definitely interesting, but the food is what keeps this restaurant hopping. Start off with a large, hot, fresh cinnamon roll: flakey like a croissant, shaped more like a towering muffin—and delicious.

The San Marcos Café prepares a wonderful eggs Benedict entrée. The Eggs San Marcos (flour tortilla-wrapped eggs served with beans, chile, and guacamole under melted cheese) are also very good, as is the corned beef hash with potatoes. The *machaca*, which is a combination of beef, eggs, and fresh *pico de gallo*, is flavorful and filling. A nice New Mexico touch is that instead of a sprig of parsley you have fresh cilantro garnishing your plate.

The Specials board found in the main room is often filled with everything from simple pork chops and eggs to eggs Florentine.

There is a reason you need a reservation—the food is that good.

Recommended Reading: *Cerrillos Yesterday, Today and Tomorrow: The Story of a Won't Be Ghost Town* by Jacqueline E. Lawson is a loving history of Cerrillos from the time of the Pueblos to recent events. Photo illustrations from past and present give a visual timeline of boom, bust, and daily town life. The real treats found in this book are the local stories that have a small town gossipy feel.

After Breakfast: From the San Marcos Café, head south to the old town of Cerrillos. Check out the Cerrillos Turquoise Mining Museum and Casa Grande Trading Post. These are run by Todd and Patricia Brown, who have dedicated themselves to preserving the history of Cerrillos. www.casagrandetradingpost.com

Tecolote Café

1203 Cerrillos Road
Santa Fe, NM 87505
(505) 988-1362
www.tecolotecafe.com

Breakfast Hours:
Tuesday-Sunday 7am-2pm
Kid Component:***
Prices: $$

When you walk into the Tecolote Café, the first thing you notice are the owls: owl paintings, owl statues, owl drawings by customers' children, owls made from shells…lots of owls. The owls are a nod to the café's name. The café is named after the northern New Mexican town Tecolote, and the word *tecolote* means "owl" in Nahuatl (Aztec Indian).

After observing the owl décor, you might notice the sign declaring "No Toast!" but don't worry, there's plenty of breakfast bread to be had. Tecolote offers fresh baked items including muffins, biscuits, tortillas, and specialty breads, so who would want boring old toast anyway?

A bustling friendly place painted a bright white with cheerful yellow trim, the Tecolote Café is teeming with northern New Mexico hospitality. Its laid-back atmosphere draws a wide cross-section of Santa Feans, a diverse crowd of old New Mexico families, transplants, college students, and visitors.

As you venture further into the building, you'll see the eclectic art on the walls isn't limited to owls. Unicorns done in needlepoint and wildlife photos are some of the wonderful pictures you may be seated beneath. But don't get too distracted; it will take all your attention to decide what to eat from the menu brimming with options to suit a broad taste.

Some of our favorites are the *piñon-atole* pancakes, granola with yogurt and fresh fruit, and delicious French toast made from a scrumptious variety of fresh baked breads. Okay, technically,

French toast *is* toast, but they do serve it (and you will be glad they do). Tecolote offers a sizable selection of traditional New Mexican breakfasts such as burritos, *huevos rancheros*, and (if you are feeling especially adventurous) Chicken Livers Tecolote. In addition, they have traditional breakfast fare including pancakes and omelets. The menu even offers some tempting healthy breakfast adaptations with egg substitute, reduced fat, and reduced salt. If you are dining with a younger companion, the eight-item children's menu (which includes chocolate chip pancakes) will be of interest.

One the truly delightful additions to a hearty Tecolote breakfast is the bakery basket that accompanies a breakfast entrée. Spread the delicious jam that comes with the bakery basket on its variety of biscuits and muffins, and you'll almost forget about your meal. On Sundays the baskets contain sweet cinnamon rolls that are worth the trip alone.

Open and owned by the same family since 1980, Tecolote Café is a Santa Fe standard. The friendliness of the staff is genuine and the food is a wonderful treat. For a place to meet friends or just read the paper over breakfast, make Tecolote a stop on your trip to Santa Fe.

Recommended Reading: Ana Howland lives on a dirt road with her daughter and controlling husband in *The Road from La Cueva* (a first place winner in the 2008 New Mexico Book Awards) by Sheila Ortego. Ana contemplates how things have gone wrong as she reshapes her life in an attempt to recapture her dreams. This deeply human novel is a meditation on self and courage.

After Breakfast: We like to head south down Cerrillos Road to an off-the-beaten-path destination, Stephen's Consignment Gallery. Stephen's is a large wandering store filled with high-end art, furniture, and antiques. Drifting carefully through this narrow-aisled store you will wonder where these beautiful treasures have spent their lives up until this point, and you may end up purchasing a unique keepsake.
www.stephensconsignments.com

Tesuque Village Market

599 Bishop's Lodge Road
Santa Fe, NM 87501
(505) 988-8848

Breakfast hours:
Daily 7am–11am
Kid Component:***
Prices: \$\$

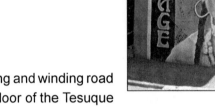

It is a long and winding road to the door of the Tesuque Village Market, but it is one of the most beautiful drives you can make for breakfast in the Santa Fe area. In order to be in the proper mood when you arrive for this dining experience, you should avoid the mean rush of Highway 84/285 and take the leisurely drive to Tesuque from Santa Fe on Bishop's Lodge Road. The road will guide you past beautiful old adobe homes tucked behind coyote fencing, horses grazing in open green fields, and giant cottonwood trees. Drivers and passengers alike will be happy and at peace when you arrive amidst the morning hustle and bustle of the Market.

Worn wooden floors will welcome you at the threshold of the Market. The floors are so remarkable, it is impossible not to think about the many shoes that have walked across them. We saw ranchers in their cowboy boots, hikers in their hiking shoes, and little kids in their flip-flops.

As soon as you walk into the market in your own personal footwear, you will be greeted by mouthwatering cinnamon rolls, fine desserts, and fresh bread. The pastries may be hollering your name, but try to ignore their pleas. Grab a menu from the front table and find yourself a seat in this cozy well-loved restaurant where you can enjoy a full breakfast.

There are several seating options available. Sitting inside, you will feel the pleasant hum of this busy eatery. Dishes clank and the cash register rings amid the murmur of conversations in English and Spanish. Outside seating is also an option, even as the weather cools down in the fall and winter. The Market has large heaters on the front porch, and sitting out there allows you some prime people-watching opportunities. Slow moving cars, pedestrians, tall dogs, and bicycle riders are part of the moving landscape on view from the front porch.

With all the atmosphere and activity, it might be easy to miss the outstanding food flowing out of the kitchen, but the food at the Market is worth your undivided attention. The *huevos rancheros* with blue corn tortillas are a highlight. While you have the option of red or green chile, we recommend the red. It is rich, thick, not too hot, and not too mild. We also have enjoyed the breakfast burrito and the croissant sandwich.

While breakfast at this market is always filling, you may still be tempted by the bakery case as you leave the restaurant. If so, stop and pick up a treat to enjoy later in the day.

Recommended Reading: Tesuque resident Andrew Leo Lovato has written a scholarly book looking deeply at Santa Fe's cultural identity in *Santa Fe Hispanic Culture: Preserving Identity in a Tourist Town.*

After Breakfast: About a half-mile from the Tesuque Village Market you will find the Shidoni Foundry and Galleries. A visit to the Foundry should include a walk through the sculpture garden and art gallery. Shidoni is a bronze foundry where artists have their works of art poured into sculpture molds. If you visit on a Saturday afternoon, you may be able to see a bronze pour in progress. Visit the foundry's website for more information on the pour schedule.
www.shidoni.com

Tía Sophia's

210 West San Francisco
Santa Fe, NM 87501
(505) 983-9880

Breakfast Hours:
Monday-Saturday 7am-11am
Price: $$
Kid Component:**

Tía Sophia's may have one of the best-kept secrets in town as it serves up some of the most authentic New Mexican food all around. The restaurant's founder, Sophia Aleck, is not a native New Mexican, but emigrated from Greece in the1930s.

Another one of Tía Sophia's greatest secrets is that it has the best booth seating in the state of New Mexico. Tall high-backed wooden booths cloak breakfast diners in private boxes that line the walls of the restaurant. The booths often inspire great conversations. As a matter of fact they inspired the conversation that began our work on this book.

There are also café tables at Tía Sophia's, and some of the tables near the windows at the front of the restaurant allow for fun tourist watching as people wend their way down San Francisco Street. The reality of eating at Tía Sophia's, however, is that you can't be too picky about where you are sitting—just be glad you got inside the door and get to try this magnificent food. Even on weekdays there is likely to be a short wait for a table, but all waiting is well worth your time.

If you find yourself waiting for a table, stroll across the street to Santa Fe's historic Lensic Theater where Rita Hayworth, Roy Rogers, and Judy Garland performed in the theater's early years.

The walls at Tía's are decorated with glittery sombreros, big baskets, woolen Mexican rugs, and vintage Fiesta dresses adorned with row upon row of fancy braid and rickrack. If measured, the rickrack on these skirts would probably reach all the way to Tesuque!

Tía Sophia's menu warns all breakfasters, "not responsible for too hot chile." The chile is hot, but good! The menu is filled with great breakfast selections plus daily specials, which might include: two eggs on a flour tortilla; a quesadilla with eggs, bacon, and cheese; and a breakfast burrito with *chorizo*, cheese, potatoes, and chile. Other regular breakfast items include a breakfast burrito with your choice of meat, an omelet made your way, eggs and toast with an option for red or green chile and/or salsa, or cereal. We highly recommend visiting Tía Sophia's on Friday and ordering the Friday Special: eggs your way with a blue corn rolled enchilada served with beans, toast, and jam. Enchiladas for breakfast are fabulous. We also adored Tía's *posolé*. It brought tears to our eyes, tasting just like grandpa's homemade *posolé*.

Recommended Reading: For a clever twist on childhood favorite *The Little Red Hen*, look for *The Little Brown Roadrunner* by Leon Wender. The title character grows corn instead of wheat, ending up with tortillas! And she does it all herself, since pals Jackrabbit, Coyote, and Horny Toad won't help.

After Breakfast: Plan to do some book browsing and shopping at a great local bookstore right down the street. Collected Works Bookstore specializes in New Mexico history and architecture, Native American art, New Mexico guidebooks, New Mexican cooking, and books by local authors.
www.collectedworksbookstore.com

Tortilla Flats

3139 Cerrillos Road
Santa Fe NM 87507
www.tortillaflats.net

Breakfast Hours:
Daily 7am-5pm
Kid Component: ***
Prices: $$

Are you a person who pays attention to things like the Surgeon General's warning on cigarette packages, and "possible side effects" on medicine bottles? Then be sure and heed the warning on Tortilla Flats' menu: "We are not responsible if the Chile is too hot! "

It's not necessary to get up with *el gallo rojo* to enjoy the New Mexican cuisine here. Breakfast is served until 5:00pm. Be sure to remember what you order, because if the word "smothered" is in the description, you may not recognize your tamale, burrito, or *huevos rancheros* under all that (red or green) chile. Don't hesitate to request your chile on the side.

The "Tortilla Flats Breakfast Special" consists of hash browns topped with two eggs, ham, sausage, or bacon with a blend of white cheddar and jack cheese on a folded tortilla, smothered with red or green chile. It's a good choice for a first-timer. Several breakfast dishes are served with salsa on the side, and the salsa is fabulous.

A friend of ours swears by "El Tamale," which comes with two eggs any style, smothered (there's that word again!) with red or green chile and beans, served with corn or flour tortillas. (And yes, there's a tamale too!) The "create your own omelet" options and an extensive a la carte section allow the diner almost infinite variety. The "Our Own Recipes" traditional pancakes with blueberries are delicious. Six inches in diameter, with a blueberry in every bite, they're accompanied by hot syrup.

Tortilla Flats is a local favorite and tends to be busy, but you will rarely have to wait for a table. Extra parking is available in the nearby bowling alley lot. You'll see lots of folks reading the *Santa Fe New Mexican* ("The West's Oldest Newspaper, Serving Santa Fe and Northern New Mexico since 1849"), which they may have purchased from one of many vendors who sell papers on the fly at busy intersections around town. The paper is also available from a machine outside the restaurant, but the machine often sells out early in the day.

Both tables and booths are available in three separate dining areas. Families dining with children will find plenty of room for high chairs and a nice breakfast menu for kids.

Recommended Reading: Nobody could have predicted the weather *The Day it Snowed Tortillas/El día que nevaron tortillas*. This bilingual collection of folktales is by Santa Fe resident Joe Hayes, one of America's premier storytellers.

After Breakfast: Many New Mexico scholars and authors have done research at the New Mexico State Records Center and Archives and the New Mexico State Library. These agencies share a building just off Cerrillos Road at 1209 Camino Carlos Rey. Open weekdays only.
www.nmcpr.state.nm.us/
www.nmstatelibrary.org

Zia Diner

326 South Guadalupe
Santa Fe, NM
(505) 988-7008 87501
www.ziadiner.com

Breakfast Hours:
Daily 7am-11am
Kid Component: **
Prices: $$

The zia symbol originates from the ancient symbols found at Zia Pueblo in New Mexico. The symbol can be found all over the state, and most prominently on New Mexico's state flag. The symbol represents the sun, the four seasons, four directions, and the four stages of human life. The people of Zia Pueblo also believed that people have four sacred obligations; a person must develop a strong body, clear mind, pure spirit, and a devotion to the community. The Zia Diner may help you prepare for these obligations.

The Zia Diner is located half a mile west of the Plaza. For visitors staying near the Plaza, it is a walk, but plenty of parking should be available during breakfast hours. It is easy to spend a significant amount of time enjoying coffee and breakfast in the relaxed atmosphere of this modern art deco diner with a New Mexico touch. Take note of the thunderbird sconces on the walls and the metal artwork above the bar. Diner walls are hung with local artists' paintings.

Comfortable booths and café tables allow for intimate conversation and larger group dining. The Zia Diner has wireless access, so bring your laptop, but don't let it distract you from the amazing food.

Walking in the door of the Zia Diner you will find yourself satisfied. To the right, just inside the entrance sits a case filled with tempting and beautiful pastries, perfect for a breakfast on the go. Sit-down breakfast options include cereals for the light eater and asparagus omelets for the more adventurous diners.

Zia Diner is known for its comfort food home cooking. In order to provide something for everyone's comfort, the breakfast menu includes eggs and grits and a chicken-fried steak with eggs. Zia also has New Mexico's traditional breakfast burrito. The menu also includes exciting twists on the New Mexico breakfast palette with *huevos machaca* (shredded beef with eggs, hash browns, jalapeños, and pinto beans), and the nutty New Mexican (eggs Benedict with green chile and corned beef hash on an English muffin).

We can recommend the breakfast burrito if you want a highly traditional New Mexico breakfast without any surprises. Red and green chile is usually mild compared with other restaurants in Santa Fe. Zia uses Taos farm eggs in all of its egg dishes. The menu states the eggs are "from natural, grain-fed, free-roaming, life-loving chickens."

Recommended Reading: Learn more about the zia symbol in famed New Mexico author Rudolfo Anaya's *Zia Summer*, the first of four mystery novels featuring private detective Sonny Baca.

After Breakfast: Once you've feasted on Zia Diner's great food, step over to the Santa Fe Depot, the end (or the beginning) of the line for New Mexico's newest train, the Rail Runner. As a passenger, listen for the familiar cartoon roadrunner "beep-beep" just before the train starts to roll. The Rail Runner route goes from Santa Fe to Belen, with lots of stops along the way, providing a unique scenic vantage point of both rural and urban New Mexico.
www.nmrailrunner.com/

Santa Rosa

Route 66 Restaurant

1819 Will Rogers Dr.
Santa Rosa, NM 88435
(575) 472-9925

Breakfast Hours:
Daily 7am-11am
Kid Component:**
Prices: $

Picture it: a restaurant named for Old Route 66, located on Old Route 66, in a small town on Old Route 66. The walls are covered with Route 66 memorabilia including postcards, license plates, photos of old cars and works by local artists. Elvis seems to be someone's favorite because he is also featured on the walls.

"The Route," as this restaurant is called by locals, serves up favorite breakfast dishes daily. The most popular platter is *huevos rancheros* served with beans, hash browns, and a flour tortilla. In addition, hot cakes, chops and eggs, French toast, steak and eggs, cinnamon toast, and oatmeal are available—not to mention omelets made with cheese, green chile and ham. Other menu choices include eggs with corned beef hash, biscuits with sausage gravy, a sausage/egg smothered burrito, and a variety of hand-held breakfast burritos. The popular hand-held burritos are regularly ordered as take-out by Santa Rosa residents on the go.

The Route offers a warm atmosphere and lots of flavor.

Recommended Reading: Famed New Mexico author Rudolfo Anaya was born in Pastura, a small village on the plains near Santa Rosa. His acclaimed novel *Bless Me, Ultima* is about a six-year-old boy growing up in New Mexico. The story told in the novel takes place in the vicinity of Santa Rosa.

After Breakfast: Devoted fans can turn a visit to Santa Rosa into an Anaya pilgrimage. The *Bless Me, Ultima* Rudolfo Anaya Sculpture Park dedicated in March, 2008 is at the north entrance to Park Lake off Historic Route 66 in Santa Rosa. In addition to bronze sculptures, the park features a natural stone waterfall and a shallow pool with a golden carp tile mosaic. In 2004 Anaya donated the desk he used for 37 years (the desk at which he wrote *Bless Me, Ultima*) to the Moise Memorial Library of Santa Rosa. It's definitely worth the trip to the library (208 South 5th Street) to read Anaya's touching letter describing his feelings and hopes for the desk. www.santarosanm.org

La Familia

503 Hudson Street
Silver City, NM 88061
(575) 538-2251

Breakfast Hours: Tuesday-
Sunday 6:30am-11:30am
Prices: $$
Kid Component:***

Our haunt for *huevos rancheros* in Silver City is La Familia Restaurant, across from the post office on Highway 90, heading south towards Tyrone. Just as a rose is a rose is a rose, one could say *huevos rancheros* are *huevos rancheros* are *huevos rancheros*. Not so; ambiance has a lot to do with the enjoyment and pleasure of *huevos rancheros*. The context is important.

The décor at La Familia is 1950-ish, just this side of "Happy Days" without the juke-box. Some of the vinyl booth seats are cracked, but that's part of the charm of the place.

The service is impeccable. We almost always get seated on arrival, but occasionally there is a wait. La Familia is full of "down home" culinary fragrance and the sussurant sounds of life.

The fare is varied: from pancakes to pork chops with eggs. Servers deliver the plates nice-'n'-hot promptly from the kitchen and hover to keep coffee cups full. While sitting in the restaurant you will be surrounded by conversations in English and Spanish, and occasionally French. From the kitchen you may hear the just audible sound of a radio tuned to a Spanish-language station playing *musica ranchera* (Mexican folk music). *Aqui hay vida* (the place is lively).

Importantly, the cooks at La Familia don't gussy-up the food with fancy sauces or fancy names. The servers make sure you get what you want and answer questions about the spiciness of the choices. They all speak English, and most of them speak Spanish.

La Familia is part of a long legacy of Mexican restaurants in Silver City. Until a few years ago, the site boasted a restaurant called Geronimo's. In 2006 Luis and Diane Dominguez bought the business and gave the restaurant its current name. There are loads of Mexican restaurants in Silver City and lots of restaurants that are not, strictly speaking, Mexican restaurants but serve Mexican food. La Familia gets an "A" for breakfast New Mexico style.

Recommended Reading: *New Mexico Place Names: A Geographical Dictionary* edited by Thomas M. Pearce is a font of information about the origins of New Mexico place names.

After Breakfast: The Gila National Forest is the site of the famous Gila Cliff Dwellings, carved out of the face of an escarpment by the Mogollon, a people who inhabited the area more than 700 years ago. The Cliff Dwellings are two hours north of Silver City.
www.nps.gov/gicl

Grinder Mill

403 W College Ave
Silver City, NM 88061
(575) 538-3366

Breakfast hours:
Daily 5am-9pm
Kid component:**
Price: $

The Grinder Mill opened in 1979 and is known locally as "the brown bag place." It is possible to eat at this restaurant, but many locals call in their orders so they can just grab and go, thus "the brown bag place."

One of the most wonderful things about The Grinder Mill is its location. It is about three doors down from the Silver City Public Library and within walking distance of Western New Mexico University's Miller Library. The restaurant is located in the heart of Silver City's downtown; an area filled with historic buildings, art galleries, and unique gift shops.

The menu includes a small variety of Mexican and American food. Traditional breakfasts include biscuits and gravy; hotcakes; and eggs, bacon, and hash browns served with a tortilla or toast.

The great service, convenient location, and economical prices make this restaurant a great stop on any Silver City visit.

Recommended Reading: Explore the Gila Wilderness with Mark Salmon in *Gila Descending: A Southwestern Journey*. Salmon recounts his travels on his 200-mile Gila River journey in this gripping story. To keep him company on his real-life adventure he brings along his faithful dog and wandering cat.

After Breakfast: Plan a visit to the Catwalk, about an hour and a half north of Silver City on Highway 180. This National Scenic Trail area offers opportunities for hiking, fishing, and wildlife viewing.
www.silvercity.org/dest_catwalk.shtml

Manzanares Street Coffeehouse

110 Manzanares Street
Socorro, NM 87801
(575) 838-0809
www.socorrocoffee.com

Breakfast hours:
Daily 7am-6pm
Kid component:*
Price: $$

You know you have found the right place to buy coffee and enjoy breakfast when you hear, "I plan my trip around a stop at Manzanares when I am driving from Las Cruces to Albuquerque" and "I stopped at that coffeehouse all the time when I made trips between Tucson and Santa Fe." People love this place, and the coffee is worthy of the rave reviews.

The Manzanares Street Coffeehouse is fun and funky and its location in central New Mexico is an important stop whether you live in Socorro, are staying in town for several days, or are just passing though. You will find this cozy restaurant just minutes off of Interstate 25. Manzanares has a bright whimsical mural that is easy to spot on the west side as you travel down California Street. The mural includes images of people riding bikes, the Socorro Mountains, and a man happily soaking in a bath of hot coffee. All of the people depicted in the mural are living local characters that you may spot on your visit to the Manzanares Street Coffeehouse.

We felt especially welcomed on one of our recent visits when we discovered there was a decaf coffee waiting for us. The coffee's name: "Librarian Blend." The coffee included this description: "This blend is representative of the soul of the librarian: steady, reassuring, and always there with that slight edge of eccentricity. It has a bold base with a bit of sparkle. Here's to good reading." We sampled all of the coffee available during our visit, and this, of course, was our favorite.

The greatness of the coffee served at Manzanares is only rivaled by the wonderful food. In this restaurant you may walk in through the front or side door and place your order at the front counter. The wait staff will deliver your entrée to you, hot from the kitchen. The menu includes several scrambled egg sandwiches served with your choice of toppings. The New Mexican is a sandwich with eggs, cheese and green chile. The Tomato Sandwich comes with eggs, cheese, and a fresh red tomato. Both of these dishes come highly recommended.

The menu also includes a large selection of omelets. On the lighter side, we can also recommend the oatmeal (which is served in a giant coffee cup) and the yogurt and granola.

Manzanares is filled with lots of comfortable seating. You may choose to sit at a small table and read a book or relax on a comfortable couch to chat with a friend. The walls of the restaurant are lined with artwork by local artisans. Large windows look out onto Manzanares Street where, just around the corner, you will find the historic Socorro Plaza.

Recommended Reading: Authors who write about the western United States share their passions, secrets, and inspirations in *Hot Coffee and Cold Truth: Living and Writing the West* edited by W. C. Jameson.

After Breakfast: The coffee at Manzanares is served in honor of Socorro's great librarians. Meet some of the librarians in town when you visit the Socorro Public Library and the New Mexico Tech Skeen Library.
www.adobelibrary.org
infohost.nmt.edu/~nmtlib

Sofia's Kitchen

105 Bullock Ave.
Socorro, NM 87801
(575) 835-0022

Breakfast Hours:
Daily 7am-9pm
Kid Component:***
Price: $

In doing the research for our breakfast books, we've had more than our share of chile. We admit that we enjoy the flavor of both red and green, and we even like to think of ourselves as chile fanciers. We've used words such as zesty, zippy, lively, racy, tangy, and spicy to describe chile. But after a few bites of the offerings at Sofia's Kitchen, we knew we'd be heading back to the thesaurus to find a whole new level of adjectives, perhaps including high octane, incendiary, or even where's-the-nearest-fire-extinguisher?

Okay, maybe it was foolhardy to order the breakfast burrito and specify *chorizo* as our breakfast meat of choice (instead of ham, bacon or sausage). At least we had the presence of mind to order the green chile on the side instead of "smothered" as listed on the menu.

As for a description of the *chorizo* and the green chile, let's just say that they are definitely not for wimps. Accordingly, we're thinking of subtitling this review Diary of a Wimpy Chile Fancier. And in case you're wondering, we don't know of a single incidence of spontaneous combustion that can be traced to Sofia's cuisine.

Breakfast plates are served all day, and come with hash browns, or beans and toast, or tortillas unless otherwise noted. The *huevos rancheros* can be made with either corn or flour tortillas and are excellent. Steak and eggs, chicken fried steak and eggs, a variety of omelets (including the New Mexico one containing jalapeños, onions, cheese, and mushrooms), pancakes, French toast, and biscuits and gravy should satisfy the appetite of folks who prefer a non-chile experience. We have friends who will attest to this. We observed multi-generational families occupying some of the larger tables and everyone seemed to be enjoying the food and congenial atmosphere. Maybe the ancestral photos gazing down from the family tree painted on one wall had something to do with that.

Recommended Reading: Hired to plan a grandiose new visitors' center, PR maven extraordinaire Sasha Solomon travels to every local point of interest (and deals with a major family crisis) in *The Socorro Blast* by Pari Noskin Taichert.

After Breakfast: Taking a cue from the mural on the wall at Sofia's; head to Very Large Array (VLA) where you will find 27giant dish antennas of the Very Large Array radio telescope on the nearby Plains of San Agustin, 50 miles west of Socorro.
www.vla.nrao.edu.

Doc Martin's Restaurant

125 Paseo del Pueblo Norte
Taos, NM 87571
(575) 758-1977
www.taosinn.com/
restaurant.html

Breakfast hours: Monday-
Friday 7:30am-11am,
Saturday-Sunday 7:30am-2pm
Kid Component:*
Prices: $$

Sitting in the middle of town, steps from the Taos plaza, Doc Martin's Restaurant at the Taos Inn lies physically and historically at the crossroads of Taos.

A real person, Doctor Martin was the only doctor in Taos when he arrived in the late 1800s. The building that was his home now houses Doc Martin's Restaurant, and is surrounded by other historic Taos homes that make up what is today the Taos Inn. Martin's wife was an artist, and the couple entertained local artists in their home. The Taos Society of Artists was founded in 1912 by Bert Phillips and Ernest Blumenschein in the Martin dining room.

Entering the restaurant, you will be guided through low arched doorways into the cozy dining room. Wrought iron chandeliers hang from the wood ceilings. If you are seated in the bar room, take note of the carvings in the bar and the ceiling. The room has a northern New Mexico style with a pinch of warmth from the Pacific Northwest.

Doc Martin's restaurant is an important crossroads of activities and events even today. You will find local Taoseños and world travelers dining side-by-side. While dining in this special location, you might overhear a famous artist advising a student about her art career, a movie director discussing his current film location, politicians debating solutions to local crime issues, and tourists planning their day at Taos Pueblo.

While the colorful people and bubbles of conversation provide entertainment, the food at Doc Martin's restaurant is flawless. Menu highlights include the breakfast burrito, with a side of sour cream and pinto beans and the eggs Benedict, with a side of potatoes and fresh fruit. Pancakes, French toast, and bakery baskets are also available. The weekend brunch fare is a little more extensive than a traditional breakfast menu and includes items such as soups, sandwiches, and salads.

Parking for the restaurant is available in a small lot behind the hotel. Look for the blue neon Taos Inn sign as you are traveling down Paseo del Pueblo Norte, and turn into the narrow alley adjacent to the hotel. Weekends at Doc Martin's can be busy. Call ahead to make reservations if you are on a tight schedule.

Recommended Reading: Read more about the artist colonies in Taos and Santa Fe by checking out *Taos and Santa Fe: The Artist's Environment 1982–1942* by Van Deren Coke.

After Breakfast: Take a leisurely walk over to the Harwood Gallery on Ledoux Street. Established by the Taos Society of Artists, the Harwood Gallery collects and exhibits artwork from the early 1900s to the present. www.harwoodmuseum.org

Michael's Kitchen

304 C N. Pueblo Road
Taos, NM 87571
(575) 758-4178
www.michaelskitchen.com

Breakfast Hours:
Daily 7am-8:30pm
Kid Component:**
Prices: $$

You know a restaurant must either be excellent or crazy to include a line of patrons waiting for breakfast as part of their logo. Michael's Kitchen is one of Taos' excellent breakfast stops, and it proudly promotes the long lines of patrons waiting for a table that snake out the door all day and every day.

The sweet smell of a bakery will draw you quickly from the busy parking lot to the end-of-the-line of breakfast anticipation. The line, in fact, is so long and filled with such a mixture of people, it develops its own culture. As you stand in line on a typical morning you will find yourself among tottering grandmothers, tough leathered Harley Davidson riders, local families, and chattering tourists who are concerned about their decision to commit to this particular breakfast experience. Standing in line at Michael's is not time wasted. Enjoy the company and take the opportunity to start a conversation with someone standing near you. You may make a new friend or find out the "real story" behind a *Taos News* headline.

The owners of Michael's have enclosed a special standing area for patrons (especially appreciated in the colder months). The standing area affords a great view of the street life on Taos' old main street.

The wait—yes it is worth it! The food served out of Michel's Kitchen is outstanding and the menu is quite extensive with food for every taste. *Huevos rancheros* come highly recommended by locals. Other New Mexico breakfast fare includes the breakfast burrito, the breakfast enchilada, and hash browns with chile. Omelets are available in at least five different varieties.

Michael's Kitchen is also a bakery, so the line of sweet foods you can order is as extensive as the line going out the door. Muffins, croissants, fritters, fruit-filled burritos, pecan rolls, cookies, and cinnamon rolls are just a few examples.

Sitting in the restaurant you can enjoy the hum of the energetic activity surrounding you. Old wooden booths and well-worn wooden tables and chairs will make you feel comfortably at home. Stained glass windows and lace curtains finish off the comfort of a home-cooked breakfast.

When you go to Michael's, go to enjoy the atmosphere of the people you will find in line, but stay in line to enjoy the fiesta of food.

Recommended Reading: In *The Great Taos Bank Robbery: And Other Indian Country Affairs,* Tony Hillerman writes about a bearded lady standing in line at a bank, apparently preparing to rob the bank. This story and other essays found in the book tell the tales of New Mexico and its eccentricities.

After Breakfast: Taos Pueblo, occupied for nearly 1000 years, is just down the road from Michael's Kitchen. Visitors may take tours of this historic pueblo and have the opportunity to purchase art and food from local residents. The pueblo is open to tourists daily but closes for tribal celebrations and rituals. Check the website before planning your visit. www.taospueblo.com

Kix on 66 Coffee Shop and Eatery

1102 East Route 66 Blvd.
Tucumcari, NM 88401
(575) 461-1966
www.kixon66.com

Breakfast Hours: Daily 5am-2pm
Kid Component: ******
Prices: \$\$

Kix on 66 has been owned and operated since 1995 by Yvonne Braziel and her sister Yvette Peacock. They are also owners of another fine restaurant, Del's, just one block east of Kix. They have received many awards recognizing their business acumen: Rural Entrepreneurs of the Year, 2002; Special Recognition by the Tucumcari-Quay County Chamber of Commerce, 2004; and Business of the Year, 1996 and 1997. Yvette and Yvonne provide the Tucumcari community with great food in pleasant surroundings served by well-trained men and women.

Driving east or west on old Route 66, the landscaping of Kix on 66 catches your eye; a nice wooden fence with outdoor tables, an old wagon, and desert plants pleasantly arranged. You will also find plenty of room to park west and south of the building.

Enter the building from the west and you'll see an attractive display of "old things" as well as items to purchase. Inside the front door you will also find a glass display case with melt-in-your-mouth pastries: cinnamon rolls, assorted of doughnuts, muffins, pies, and more. Above this case are signs announcing specialty drinks: caramel macchiato, white chocolate mocha, caffe breve, espresso can panna, hot teas, icy blended beverages, milk shakes, and floats are just a few of over 20 items on the list. The servers are always patient as you study the menu for several minutes and finally ask about the special item you want to order. It is delightful to be able to tantalize yourself with these wonderful beverages.

As you make your way into the restaurant, there are several booths along the north and east walls and a counter with stools to the south. The breakfast menu includes Route 66 Favorites: corned beef hash, spicy *chorizo,* sirloin steak, bacon, ham, or sausage with two eggs, hash browns, toast or biscuits, omelets any way you like them, Kix buttery croissant, and our favorite, the breakfast *quesadilla*. The eggs in the *quesadilla* are so light over the cheese-smoothed tortilla. We like to order the *quesadilla* with fresh-made salsa. Pouring the salsa over the top of this goodness, you may find yourself saying, "it just couldn't get any better."

This restaurant represents the quintessential small town friendly restaurant. No one seems to mind when we spend time here visiting with half the town and weary travelers.

Recommended Reading: You might kick yourself if you don't read at least one of the following: *Along Route 66* by Quinta Scott; *Route 66: the Mother Road* by Michael Wallis; *Route 66 Remembered* and *Legendary Route 66: A Journey Through Time Along America's Mother Road* by Michael Witzel; *Route 66: Spirit of the Mother Road* by Bob Moore; *Route 66: Lost and Found: Ruins and Relics Revisited* by Russell Olsen; and especially for kids, *Don't Forget Winona* by Jean Whitehouse Peterson.

After Breakfast: Continue your Route 66 experience by exploring the unique buildings and signs dotting every foot of highway down Tucumcari's main street. Conclude your tour of town at the Tucumcari Convention Center on the west side of town, where you will find Tom Coffin's roadside sculpture honoring the spirit of Route 66.

Our friends and contributors who brought the perfect ingredients to the table

Paulita Aguilar is currently a reference librarian at University Libraries, University of New Mexico. Growing up at Santo Domingo Pueblo, it is no surprise that Paulita's research interests range from indigenous libraries to services to remote and rural libraries. She is also a strong proponent of increasing the number of minority/ethnic librarians. When not at the library, Paulita enjoys hiking, fly fishing, and bird watching with her husband Jim. Paulita contributed the review for the Church Street Café.

Kathy Albrecht recently retired from New Mexico Tech Library, a position which lured the Albrechts to Socorro County after her 17 years with Taos Public Library. The village of San Antonio, near Bosque del Apache National Wildlife Refuge, became home. The Albrechts are restoring an old adobe there and Kathy writes a long-running global affairs column for local newspapers. She served as an officer of the New Mexico Library Association for five years and is currently on the Rio Grande Agricultural Land Trust board. Kathy contributed the review for Acosta's Mexican Restaurant.

As a Research Librarian at the Los Alamos National Laboratory Research Library, **Donna Berg** came to New Mexico after a career working in school, public and academic libraries. She has been active in the Special Libraries Association at the local and national level and is currently a Competitive Intelligence Analyst in the Technology Transfer Division of LANL. Outside her professional life Donna is enamored of trashy novels, cross-country skiing, Palladio, her Italian bicycle, and loitering in coffee shops with other librarians. Donna contributed the review for Hot Rocks Java Café.

A resident of New Orleans for six years, **Jimmy Bevill** moved his family to New Mexico after Katrina. Born and raised a "deep southerner" in Jackson, Mississippi, Jimmy has come to appreciate and enjoy the many things that make the Southwest famous, especially the food. Jimmy currently works for Albuquerque Public Schools while bravely fighting to publish his first novel. He misses humidity more than he thought he would, and he's gradually learning folks on the many wonders of grits! Jimmy contributed the review for The Range Café and Bakery.

Donna Birchell, a Library Tech for the Carlsbad Public Library, has been eating since she was born and thought it was time to put it to good use. Writing has been a passion since age 12 when her medieval ghost story won rave reviews from her staunchest critics—her parents. Since then, she is rarely seen without a pen in her hand. On the rare occasion that she has free time, Donna enjoys beading, gourd painting, hiking, and spending time with her two sons. Donna contributed reviews for Calloway's Café, Happy's, Jack's, and Roja's Mexican Grill and Restaurant.

Leslie Broughton is Head of Collections and Instruction at New Mexico Highlands University. She has an MA in Library Science from the University of Arizona. She has an MA in Comparative Literature, a BFA, and BA from the University of New Mexico. Her previous position was the Collection Development Librarian at the Arizona Historical Society Library in Tucson. In her free time she enjoys hiking and painting in the mountains of Northern New Mexico. Leslie contributed the review for Charlie's Bakery and Café.

Susanne Caro is the State Documents Librarian at the New Mexico State Library in Santa Fe where she works to provide state documents to the 28 state depositories throughout New Mexico. In her spare time she enjoys camping, hiking, painting, collage, book creation, printmaking, and making found art sculptures. She strongly believes in interactive art which invites the viewer to touch and play with the object. She is currently working on a book of linotypes focusing on the fairies of the Southwest. Susanne contributed the review for the San Marcos Café.

Natasha Casteel is Branch Manager of Lomas Tramway Library, a branch of the Albuquerque/Bernalillo County Library System. Originally from North Carolina, Natasha has lived in Maine, New Hampshire and Arizona. A public librarian for 15 years, she is now happy to call New Mexico home. Natasha enjoys hiking in the Sandias with her husband and three dogs, as well as cooking, wine, interior design and obsessing over the Oscars. Natasha contributed the review for the Greenside Café.

Joan Chavez is a library director at the Moise Memorial Library in Santa Rosa. She has worked there for 21 years and enjoys her work tremendously. She is also a volunteer on several different committees in her community including Santa Rosa Crime Stoppers, the Guadalupe County Health Planning Board, Relay for Life, and the Santa Rosa Literacy Council. She enjoys spending time with her grandkids. Her hobbies are walking and reading. Joan contributed the review for the Route 66 Restaurant.

Lorie Christian is currently the Contract Administrator for the New Mexico Library Association. She has lived in the Albuquerque area since 1975. Two of her favorite hobbies are geocaching and eating. She tries to keep up on local eating spots to share with geocachers who are in the area for a day or a week. She also asks regional geocachers and librarians for suggestions on great places to eat while she and her husband are on geocaching trips. Lorie contributed the reviews for the Calico Café and El Camino Dining Room.

Julia Clarke is a librarian in the Albuquerque/Bernalillo County Library System. After working in academic and public libraries in North Carolina, Tennessee and Mississippi, she moved to Albuquerque because the food (except barbeque) is better. Throughout her career, she used restaurants as landmarks when providing directions to libraries. This approach results in highly satisfied—and well fed—customers. Julia contributed the review for Java Joe's.

Beverly Cooper is a Youth Librarian at Mesa Public Library in Los Alamos. She has worked there since 1996, starting in the circulation department and moving to the youth services area in 1999. Bev and her husband moved to Los Alamos in 1974 and have visited and enjoyed many restaurants in Santa Fe. Bev was born in Brooklyn but spent her growing-up years and college years in Los Angeles. She left Los Angeles on her wedding day and never returned to live although she has two grown children living there now. She is thoroughly committed to the Southwest for its beauty and diversity of cultures. Bev contributed the review for the Guadalupe Café.

Kate Garduño is a librarian at Santa Fe Community College Library, and has also worked in Albuquerque, Rio Rancho, and Pojoaque public libraries. Kate is currently training to run a half marathon and recently took

Differential Equations as a summer course. She also enjoys cross-country skiing, knitting and entertaining her dogs. Kate contributed the review for the Tecolote Café.

As director of an all-volunteer library in Capitan, **Pat Garrett** is in the midst of a second career. Having retired from the public school system in California in 1997, she and her husband spent a year building a home just west of Capitan. In the fall of 1998 needing something to do, she volunteered for a four hour shift with the Capitan Public Library. When the director passed away suddenly in the late 90s, she agreed to take the directorship for six months. Eight years later—the temporary job has become permanent. Free time is limited; she does enjoy baking, reading, and working in her yard. Pat contributed the review for the Smokey Bear Restaurant.

Amy E. Helfritz is the Librarian for Apollo College in Albuquerque. She also owns The Ambiance Studio, which creates customized artwork and photography for homes and businesses. She has received local and national recognition for her artwork. Amy loves to read (of course!), travel, and learn. She holds a Master's Degree in Education, enjoys salsa dancing, and is currently working hard to complete her first novel. Visit Amy's website at www.theambiancestudio.com to view some of her latest work. Amy contributed the review for Satellite Coffee.

Peg Johnson is the Director of Libraries at the College of Santa Fe and has been with the College for 12 years. Her favorite parts of librarianship are interacting with students to discover unexpected sources for research and convincing people that Google and Wikipedia are not all there is. Outdoor adventures with her husband and three grown children are treasured experiences. Rediscovering the joy of playing music with others has led to playing in two bands in Santa Fe. Peg belongs to a women's reading group that has been meeting monthly for 20 years. Learning to draw and to play the cello are still dreams. Peg contributed the review for the Roadside Restaurant.

Daria Labinsky was an adult reference librarian for seven years at the Rio Rancho Public Library. She is the co-author of five books, including the Southwest Book Award-winning *Frank Applegate of Santa Fe: Artist and Preservationist*. She is a free-lance writer, editor, and indexer. When not traveling with her family, she lives in Corrales. Daria contributed reviews for the Flying Star and Weck's.

Anne Lefkofsky is a New Mexico native, and a librarian with the Albuquerque/Bernalillo County Library System. Her career has included positions with Fort Bend County Libraries in Richmond, Texas and the New Mexico State Library. She is a former president of the New Mexico Library Association. Along with seeking out the ideal breakfast burrito (green inside and potatoes are must haves...), Anne continues to be on the look-out for the perfect glass of iced tea, the best local photo op, and the book (novel or nonfiction) that explains it all. Anne contributed the review for Garcia's Kitchen.

Beth Nieman is public services librarian at Carlsbad Public Library in Carlsbad where she has worked since 2001. She writes a weekly book column for the local newspaper. She serves on the Land of Enchantment Book Award committee for the New Mexico Library Association. In her spare time she enjoys reading, writing, cooking, quilt-making, and playing a number of musical instruments, including piano, organ, flute, recorder, banjo, and harpsichord. She and her husband Bob have three children. Beth contributed reviews for The Blue House Bakery and Café and the Pecos River Café.

Eileen O'Connell manages the San Pedro branch of the Albuquerque/ Bernalillo County Library System. She considers herself fortunate to be working in the neighborhood where she grew up, managing the library where she worked as a Page over 20 years ago. Keeping up with the information and leisure needs of a dynamic neighborhood takes most of her time. She spends her spare time reading, eating out, staying connected with a large and scattered family, writing, and playing with computer graphics programs. Eileen contributed the review for Christy Mae's.

Claire Odenheim has lived in Las Cruces since 1979, and before that lived in Alexandria, Virginia; Medellin, Colombia; San Juan, Puerto Rico; and Mexico City. Originally from the Detroit area, she was educated at Michigan State University (BA in Spanish and History) and the University of Michigan (MALS in Library Science). She also has an MA in Education from New Mexico State University. Claire retired in 2001 from the public schools. She was the Librarian at Gadsden High School and later the

District Library Coordinator. She also worked as Librarian at Zia Middle School and Oñate High School in Las Cruces. From 2002 to 2006 she was the librarian at the New Mexico Farm and Ranch Heritage Museum where she currently volunteers. Claire contributed reviews for Dick's Café, Spirit Winds, Mesilla Valley Kitchen, and Red Mountain Café.

Felipe de Ortego y Gasca is an award-winning writer and journalist. He is Scholar in Residence at Western New Mexico University where he is also Faculty Advisor to *The Mustang*, the university's student newspaper. He is a well-traveled gourmand who has dined in all but one of the United States, Canada, Mexico, Latin and South America, the Caribbean, England and all of Europe, the Levant countries, and North Africa. While he was Associate Editor of *La Luz Magazine* (1972-1982) the first national Hispanic public affairs magazine in English, he contributed a column on La Cocina Latina or The Happy Cooker. Felipe contributed the review for La Familia.

Mark Pendleton is Outreach Librarian at Thomas Branigan Memorial Library in Las Cruces. He writes two newspaper columns, one in the local Sunday paper and another in a monthly arts and culture paper. Mark hosts the library book club, reads in two bilingual 4th grade classes every week, does a monthly book review at a local retirement center, and facilitates two short story reading/discussion programs. Non-work interests include his family, his dog, Scrabble, reading, and trying new restaurants. Mark contributed reviews for Andele Restaurante, Enrique's Mexican Food, International Delights Café, and Milagro Coffee y Espresso.

Pam Schwarz is the Children's Librarian for The Public Library in Silver City. She has lived in New Mexico for about 17 years. Pam leads a very quiet lifestyle, spending as much time as possible with her husband and grown children. Some of her hobbies include reading, baking, and gardening. Pam contributed the review for the Grinder Mill.

Joe Sabatini recently retired after working for 41 years in New Mexico libraries. He spent the last eight years as branch manager and local history librarian at the Special Collections Library of the Albuquerque/Bernalillo County Library System, where he participated in the Albuquerque Tricentennial Celebration and the Centennial of the Albuquerque Public Library. A long-time activist for New Mexico libraries, Joe calls himself "the political operative of the New Mexico Library Association." Joe has a backyard vegetable garden, and enjoys bicycling and cultural events. Joe contributed the review for The Daily Grind.

Carol Sarath has been the Library/Media Coordinator for Gallup McKinley County Schools for more than 25 years. As such she works with all school libraries in the district, an area that covers most of McKinley County. She makes sure that students have access to as many good books as possible. Breakfast is her favorite meal to eat out but lunch and dinner come in as a close second. Carol contributed reviews for Earl's Restaurant and El Rancho Hotel and Restaurant.

Larry Sims moved to Las Vegas in 1991 when he began work at the fiberboard plant at the north end of town. Larry has been employed at New Mexico Highlands University since September 1991 to the present as a Library Automation Technician. Larry spends much of his free-time trout fishing in the Pecos Wilderness and is the Co-coordinator for Las Vegas Special Olympics. Larry contributed the review for Charlie's Bakery and Café.

Dean Smith is currently an Assistant Director of the Albuquerque/Bernalillo County Library System. Dean settled in Albuquerque in 2008 after working in New York City and London, UK. Since moving to New Mexico, finding great places to eat in the state has been a real treat. Dean contributed the review for Java Joe's.

Sabra Brown Steinsiek retired in 2003 from the University of New Mexico School of Law Library after a long career in New Mexico libraries. She is the author of four novels, including The New Mexico Book Awards 2008 Romance Winner, *Annie's Song*, and is a freelance writer for various publications. She is the editor and founder of Reading New Mexico.com, the only review site strictly for books with a New Mexico Connection. She can be reached through her website www.sabrasteinsiek.com. Sabra contributed the review for Cocina de Manuel.

Beth Aeby Teel (a.k.a. The New Mexico Troubadour) is a life-long New Mexican, and fiercely proud of it. She is a native of the Española Valley and has traveled around the country educating our fellow citizens about the wonders and joys of the 47th State. Beth spent most of 2008 in research for an upcoming young adult fiction book involving the White

House. When she isn't writing or on the road singing, reading, and telling stories, Beth spends her time as a volunteer with local hospice patients, Friends of the Española Public Library, and a hand bell choir. Visit Beth at: www.newmexicotroubadour.org. Beth contributed reviews for Angelina's Restaurant , Jo Ann's Ranch O Casados Restaurant, and the Lovin' Oven Bakery Shoppe.

Laurie Treat is a Librarian-Teacher at Aztec High School, located in Aztec. She has also taught high school U.S. History and Economics at Bloomfield High School. She is a member of New Mexico Library Association, Association of School Libraries-Special Interest Group, American Library Association, American Association for School Librarians and has worked to establish New Mexico Reads, a reading and literacy campaign sponsored by NMLA. Laurie hopes to learn to quilt and enjoys reading, sewing, cooking, and traveling. Learn more about New Mexico Reads at: www. nmla.org/NM_Reads/NM_Reads.html. Laurie contributed the review for The Main Street Bistro.

Barbara VanDongen is the District Library Coordinator for Albuquerque Public Schools. Barbara is also a Trustee of the New Mexico Library Foundation. She devotes much of her waking energy to advocating for New Mexico libraries. Barbara spends what free time she has left gardening, reading, and attending cultural events such as museum shows, the opera, and the symphony. Barbara collaborated on her review with her husband **Richard VanDongen**, a retired professor from the College of Education at UNM.. Barbara and Richard contributed the review for Barelas Coffee House.

Laddie Ward is a National Board Certified Teacher/Librarian at the new JFK Middle School in Gallup. Moving into a beautiful new space kept her busy this fall. Her favorite pastimes include family, reading (as any good librarian should), genealogy, and of course, eating out. Laddie contributed reviews for Aurelia's Diner and El Rancho Hotel and Restaurant.

Paula White is the supervisor at the Rural Bookmobile East, which provides free public library service to rural communities. This bookmobile, based in Tucumcari, is one of three in the state that is administered by the New Mexico State Library and serves the following counties: Chaves,

Curry, Eddy, Lincoln, Otero, Quay, Roosevelt, and part of San Miguel and Guadalupe. She has been traveling the roads of southeast New Mexico for 23 years and truly enjoys her job. When asked "What do you like about your job?" she will quickly say that meeting the people in the rural areas is the best part. Paula contributed the review for Kix on 66 Coffee Shop and Eatery.

Sherry York is a retired school librarian, reviewer, editor, conference presenter, and writer. She has published six books on multicultural literature. A part-time New Mexican, she lives in the Upper Canyon of Ruidoso, checks out numerous books from the Ruidoso Public Library, is a member of Friends of the Library, and participates in a book discussion group at the library. When she is not reading or writing, Sherry loves walking in the forest and occasionally dining out with friends. Sherry contributed the review for Jorge's Café.

Cheryl Zebrowski is the Cataloging/Systems Librarian at New Mexico Highlands University Thomas C. Donnelly Library. She started her career in technical libraries such as the Air Force and NASA. She is enjoying the diversity of projects in a small academic library. She loves reading mysteries and historical literature. She is also involved in local environmental organizations such as the Citizens Watershed Monitoring Team, and helps organize the annual SynergyFest. Cheryl contributed the review for Charlie's Bakery and Café.

Book List

190 East Palace: Robert Oppenheimer and the Secret City of Los Alamos by Jennet Conant
Hot Rocks Java Café, page 112

Albuquerque Downtown: From a Geologic Point of View—A Walking Tour of the City Center by George S. Austin
Java Joe's, page 42

Albuquerque: The Next Boomtown by Cheryl Seas Gorder
Weck's, page 50

Alburquerque by Rudolfo Anaya
Barelas Coffee House, page 20

All Aboard for Santa Fe: Railway Promotion of the Southwest, 1890s to 1930s by Victoria E. Dye
Lamy Station Café, page 132

Aloft: A Meditation on Pigeons and Pigeon-Flying by Stephen Bodio
Acosta's Mexican Restaurant, page 118

Along Route 66 by Quinta Scott
Kix on 66 Coffee Shop and Eatery, page 164

Annie's Song by Sabra Brown Steinsiek
Cocina de Manuel, page 26

Anything for Billy by Larry McMurtry
Mesilla Valley Kitchen, page 100

Best Novels and Short Stories of Eugene Manlove Rhodes, The by Frank V. Dearing, Editor
Christy Mae's, page 28

Big Gamble, The by Michael McGarrity
Smokey Bear Restaurant, page 58